Finding Bob's Glasses

Finding Bob's Glasses

A Memoir of Life, Love and Unfinished Paintings

Aileen O. Erickson
Illustrated by Helen O. Barbieri

Fresh Pond Publishing
Cambridge, Massachusetts

Finding Bob's Glasses © 2001 by Aileen O. Erickson

Fresh Pond Publishing
P.O. Box 381534
Cambridge, MA 02238-1534
orders: (800) 247-6553

Printed in the United States of America
Front cover photograph by Joseph Barbieri
Back cover drawing by Helen O. Barbieri
Interior book design by Sara Patton

Publisher's Cataloging-in-Publication
(*Provided by Quality Books, Inc.*)
Erickson, Aileen O.
Finding Bob's glasses : a memoir of life, love and unfinished paintings / Aileen O. Erickson ; illustrated by Helen O. Barbieri. — 1st ed.
p. cm.
LCCN 00-092184
ISBN 0-9701939-0-4

1. Erickson, Aileen O. 2. Artists—Massachusetts—Family relationships. 3. Family—Massachusetts.
4. Social isolation. 5. Work and family—Psychological aspects. I. Barbieri, Helen O. II. Title

ND237.E695A2 2001   759.13
QBI01-700417

*In loving memory
of my mother*

Drawings

Acknowledgments

First, I would like to thank my husband, Joseph Barbieri, who long ago suggested I write as well as paint and has patiently backed this drawn-out and intrusive project, often putting up with the computer and me in his workspace for days at a time.

Secondly, I would like to thank my three editors, especially Faith Lancereau for her guiding comments and questions on the first most difficult drafts. Without her help, I am not sure this particular work would have left the ground. Also, Fay Chandler, for her grasp of grammatical detail and her fine-tuning of thematic direction along the way; and Margaret Ellsworth, my sister, who made inspired cuts on a later edition.

Margery O. Erickson, my mother, was an astute and willing reader whenever asked and an overall supporter; Helen O. Barbieri, my daughter, lent her drawings and had faith.

I am also grateful for various contributions from numerous other people including: Amy Domini, S. Osborn Erickson, Hylton Jolliffe, Sarah Jolliffe, Cécile Mactaggart, and Belinda Rathbone.

Lastly, credit is due to the agents and publishers who read and intelligently commented on the manuscript.

One is most unsafe when
trying to be most impersonal.

– Anne Ridler,
The Faber Book of Modern Verse
Introduction, Granger edition

Foreword

Although in this book I have not used the real names of people and places, nothing else is fabricated except my interpretation, wherein my main interest lies.

Slyvia Plath's *The Bell Jar* apparently upset her mother and friends and the medical people who gave time, attention, and love during her illness yet were negatively portrayed in her "work of fiction." A foreword might have explained that the writer was seeing those "characters" through the eyes of her protagonist's sickness and gone on to express gratitude to her supporters in real life.

So I would like to thank the people in this book. I did not ask anybody's permission for inclusion, but at least three principals — my husband, daughter, and mother — knew what I was about and generously encouraged, rather than thwarted or censored, my search. If I have offended anybody, either family or friends, I hope they and other readers will understand that I am writing about truth within a certain context and time frame.

Finding Bob's Glasses

1

One winter morning when my daughter, Jane, was two years old, I was rushing to leave the apartment because I had to drop my husband, Bob, off at his studio, which was away from home back then, take Jane to her daycare center, and get to my studio early enough to find a parking space. Unfortunately, we could not find Bob's glasses. We looked everywhere, getting more and more upset. Finally, I gave up. I took off my coat and proceeded to tidy up Jane's room. In less than five minutes I found the glasses. Jane had put them on her stuffed koala bear to help it see better.

For over twenty-five years I have worked regular hours in my studio five days a week, only to find myself increasingly less able to finish paintings. One day, early this spring, with Jane in second grade, I began to write.

That was shortly after my high school asked me to give a talk on what my years there had meant to me. I decided that above all they had helped to encourage my artistic side. I planned to explain how and elaborate on the ways they contributed to my present life as a painter. I spent some time preparing. After the engagement was over, I was restless in my studio. One morning after taking Jane to school, instead of going straight to work, I returned home, climbed into bed with my clothes on, pulled the covers up to my face, and looked out at the new spring leaves. A few minutes later Bob came in from getting the newspaper and regarded me with surprise.

"What are you doing here?" he asked.

"I'm working," I said, "on my book."

In my studio I still paint, but at home I get up early to write. Writing makes it easier for me to paint. Even last fall, I had begun to apply the if-you-cannot-find-it-do-something-else approach to painting itself.

One of my paintings is of a white bowl containing a dark red polyurethane horse sitting on a rock with a stick in front of it. Almost touching the bowl's base and reflected in its glazed surface is a bracelet of plastic colored balls. Part of a cup, bottle, and another bowl edge the canvas.

Recently, Jane and I were studying the painting. She especially liked the bracelet. I remarked that I had found it the same way I had found her father's glasses long ago. She looked puzzled.

"The painting was done, but it was boring. Something was missing. I left it up to glance at now and then. At some odd moment I spotted the bracelet. I stopped whatever I was doing and painted it in next to the bowl. The missing something was found."

"What about the horse?" Jane asked. "Was the horse missing like the glasses?"

"No, the horse was different. For a long time I had wanted to paint it along with my usual cups and bowls and things. But I couldn't find the right painting. The painting was missing. Sometime after the bracelet, I added the horse."

"Then was the painting finished?"

"Again I thought so. But a few months later I removed a mirror, directly behind the bowl, which reflected both the bowl and a black embroidered cloth hanging on a distant wall."

"What did you find?"

"The empty space. Do you know what I do now when I want to paint but don't know what to paint?"

"What?"

"I don't paint. I go to my studio, but sometimes I don't paint all day. I rock in my rocking chair, hang my paintings on the walls, look at them, look out the window, take a nap, study my objects, think about objects at home, and suddenly I hit upon the right object to put in, like the bracelet; or the right object to take out, like the mirror; or the right painting for a special object, like this painting for the horse.

"I found the bracelet, the empty space, and the right painting the same way I found Daddy's glasses on your koala bear: by not looking for them!"

2

For eight and a half years I have been a mother. After Jane was born, my painting moved ahead even more slowly than usual. My last exhibition occurred shortly after her third birthday. Now, with an older child and more time and leisure available, unfinished canvases still line my studio walls.

When I first saw Jane's face with its mouth drooping after birth like her father's does when he is puzzled or discouraged, love filled me. From the beginning she has taught me. First because of herself and her life. Secondly, because I try to be an example and teacher to her. Sometimes, I look at her and see myself at her age. I look at that long-ago child with searching eyes, feeling she also holds answers to my present, as yet vague, quest. In fact, there is my whole world.

But how to proceed if I do not know what I am looking for? Here I am in the late spring of Jane's second grade year writing about unfinished paintings instead of painting. I want to write about other things too: a bridge my father built when he was a young man; how a gallery director turned my work down.

A writer should have more of a plan before writing a book, but shoulds have dominated much of my life so far in various, convoluted ways. Whether or not these pages are destined for the public, for now they are mine.

3

Last fall, I had not finished a painting in half a decade. But the canvases I labored on were heavy with layers of compositions painted over each other. Shortly after Jane began second grade, I invited a gallery director to my studio.

Over the years I had exhibited in her gallery before she was its director, and I expected to do so again, but she was not interested.

After she left, I recalled her face and voice and movements while she had looked at the work, spoken about it, moved in front of it, closer and further back. I moved as she had, her words in my head, and I looked at my paintings with her eyes until it was time for me to leave. I locked up the studio and walked to the subway, as I do two days a week when Bob drives Jane. After the subway I took the bus home. It was a normal day.

"She's probably right," I told Bob with a careless shrug, but later in the evening I went around with red, swollen eyes.

That night I dreamed that my head and legs and arms were flying off in different directions. There was no center. The next morning I walked our dog Homer, made lunches for Jane and myself, and dropped Jane at school. Then I drove to my studio. My work was still on the walls. As I walked in, the gallery director's way of looking at it faded, and my own returned.

I remember Jane taking an after-school clay class during her kindergarten year. I had expected results: a bowl painted with bright colors, a bright, shiny pitcher or cup, such as I had seen periodically on the classroom shelves. After a few classes she brought home one small, unpainted, unglazed object.

"Is it done?" I asked, as I tried to figure out what it was. A shape, like a two-inch-high candle's flame, rose from a flat, thin base. Over it fitted a removable, bowl-like form, sides only, which protected the flame and rested on the base. The clay was reddish earth color, patted, pinched, and shaped in a tactile manner.

"It's a butter churn," Jane said proudly.

"It's nice, honey," I said, secretly disappointed.

My initial reaction reminds me of a truth painful to artists. Many viewers would not appreciate that odd, dry object any more than the gallery director did my work at the time of her visit last fall. The eyes with which we look upon art are mysterious, trained or untrained.

The first years of Bob's and my marriage have passed, and Jane no longer needs me in a small child's way, but we are a close family. A dog is pleased to see me and keeps me company on my walks. My mother is a twenty-minute drive away. My siblings keep in touch by phone calls, letters, and occasional visits. My closest friends and I visit when we can find time outside the demands of our families and work. Yet in my studio I take out this, add that, until a month's, six month's, a year's work is undone, replaced by other images to eventually be undone.

I have noted that Jane's butter churn was created in a social environment. But what inspired a butter churn rather than a bowl; or spruce trees, drawn and painted on the front of a recent sculpture, rather than the trees in our neighborhood? The latter, I am convinced, came straight from my father's island in Maine, where Jane has gone for part of the summer since she was three months old.

4

While waiting to hear whether his offer to rent a large part of the island I grew up on would be accepted, my father, as a young man, built a bridge in a swampy area deep in the middle of his family's island in Maine. Recently, I heard my uncle saying it had rotted away years ago, but shortly after my father's death I found it, and since then have visited it every summer. In that part of the woods the spruce trees are spaced wide enough apart so they are easy to walk between, but as they grow older, more fall down and confuse my sense of where I am. Just when I decide I cannot find it, there it is, its domain still light-green and damp, itself covered with moss and surprisingly well built. Age or some natural trauma makes it arch and hang above the water at an odd angle, and the thick posts that hold it up slant precariously. It extends for many yards, then submerges in the swamp rather than ends.

My father was away when I was born and often absent while I was growing up. He had wanted a family of boys, three at most, but my birth brought the tally up to two girls, one boy, and me, although my younger brother followed four years later. Towards the end of his life, my father saw a photograph of small children in *Life* magazine and remarked wistfully to my mother that they reminded him of their own when small.

Isolated as he was from little children while growing up, he did not understand them nor did the demands of his business leave much time for them. When we grew older and interested him more and work exacted fewer hours, I was a teenager and rejected the intimacy that at times he seemed to desire and assume. Later, when he was close to bankruptcy and symptoms of angina manifested themselves, he began to realize his distance from us but not its cause. His bewilderment in this respect must have added to his sense of failure. Coming across the photograph, he may have wished he could go back in time and start over as a father. Or he may have thought that his children had been potentially easier to understand when small than at that present time.

Before his memorial service I put shadows under my eyes, like makeup for the stage. My father's frequent absences may have disconnected me from him at an early age, or was it something else? My older, middle sister, Susan, remembers him spanking me when I was one and a half. While trying to pull an electric cord out of the wall, I knocked a small table above me and caused a lamp with a body of red crystal to fall and break. Although my sisters and brothers were spanked from time to time, I do not believe I was, except for that once. The lesson I learned then and from my father's occasional threat of a spanking may have been this: if I stayed away from him, he would scold or spank me less.

Bob helps heal the hurt my father's absence and discipline caused me, as he never spanks Jane and is, like myself, infrequently away and then for only a few days. Also, I see now that, though I may have felt removed from my father, I did not feel unloved by him. For as long as I can remember, it was I who turned away from his occasional attempts to reach me. Three of them, although as half forgotten as the others, seem important now.

After discouraging a serious relationship of mine in college and after it fell apart, he offered to take me on a trip; I turned him down. When I was sent home from boarding school for a weekend because I plagiarized some sentences on a homework assignment, he spoke minimally to me about my misbehavior. He seemed to understand my drive for perfection and sense my shame, and be confident that in the future I would withstand the temptation to steal again. Too mortified to respond, I observed this faith in me from a distance. Over spring break a year or so later, knowing his mother had taught him to sew at an early age, I asked him to help me make a rag doll for the school fair. If the threat of bankruptcy was troubling him even then, that night he sat beside me, amused and relaxed while we worked. Later, I called from school to inform him that the doll had quickly sold.

Unaccompanied by my mother due to the family financial situation, my father took a last business trip to the Far East shortly before he died and while there made a small drawing of himself. At the bottom of the page, a lonely head stares at itself in a hotel's bedroom mirror. I forgot about the drawing soon after I saw it, but during my single years I did many such sketches of myself. Then, last summer, while helping my mother move, I came across a little calendar notebook which had belonged to my father. In each space accompanying the day's date was his handwriting, noting what he had accomplished in his work that day. "Worked on preliminary design of tank," for example, echoed the daily notations I made in a similar book, such as "Worked on bowl painting. Put in stick."

The delight I experienced in my father's company while we were making the doll stemmed from another common bond. His mind and mine, not as quick as my mother's or my siblings', could sometimes produce original work and ideas: his concept and layout of the salt operation on the island, his choice of ship to load and carry salt, and his college oil paintings of still life.

Two minds not as quick. Jane is forbidden to call anyone dumb. "That word is used too often," I tell her severely and instantly. My sister Anne used to call me dumb when I was growing up, sometimes affectionately, sometimes not, even though I did well academically. Anne did well too, but she may have felt compelled to pass her doubts onto me because Susan, next to her in age, excelled. My maternal grandfather did not call me dumb, but I suspected he thought it more seriously than Anne did. When I applied for a transfer and was accepted by the same college a smart grandchild was attending, his surprise hurt. His son-in-law, my father, was not smart either. Why else did the salt venture deplete his family's fortune for years and end in failure?

My grandfather expanded his own family's capital and generously set up trusts for his children and grandchildren, but, unlike my father, he played favorites and equated quickness of mind with worth. Not only quickness of mind. "Your father was a babe in the woods," he said to me once. Slow and innocent. If examined from a less negative point of view, that may be an accurate assessment of us both.

Although my father may not have agreed. Once, referring to a physical trait he and I had in common, he said, "Deep-set eyes are useful. Sometimes when I am in a difficult spot, I smile, and nobody can see what I am thinking. It gives me a second to look around and appraise the situation."

My father lost a fortune, but with his brothers' help he restored an island's economy. His vision of expansion is still being followed today by the company that bought him and his brothers out. The tanker, whose design he picked as the best to carry salt and to which he added cranes on deck to facilitate loading—at the time a novel idea—still operates and remains a major asset of the company. Its enlarged photograph, hanging on a wall by itself, adorns the company's top island executive's office.

The only time I saw my father paint, he worked slowly. One day, during a rare visit of his up north when I was in fourth grade, he put a vase of blue glass, the same aquamarine blue as the water that surrounded his island, on a table outside and set up an easel next to it. Slowly, painstakingly, he transferred the glass onto the canvas in such a way that the latter, unfinished and lost as it eventually was, stands out in my memory. So does the image of himself, intently focused on the vase amid the distraction and spread of the surrounding lawn, dazzling and green in spring sunshine.

And yet, just after his own father died, my father told my mother that he had felt cut off from him because he could not work with him. My grandfather was a perfectionist one step beyond his middle son, and the slow thoroughness of his work methods exhausted my father's patience. My father may have built the bridge in the woods away from the house in part to isolate himself from his parent's critical eye.

When word came through about the land, he left his parents and the unfinished bridge. I doubt if its incompletion bothered him any more than the still life's. But twenty-five years later, unfinished business on his island removed the joy from his life.

During my early adult years when I was inclined to feel more at home with nature than my best friend, I used to be comforted on my summer drives to the Maine island by a sign set slightly off the highway, stating that life was more than people. But for some time now I have tended to view my father, during those months he was building the bridge, as captive on an island governed by his father and outgrown. Nature, in the past his benefactor, even at times a temptress who lured him away from his own kind as it did me, was then part of the guard. I see him doggedly at work while encircled by high fences of closely packed spruce.

11

Most of all, I see him off by himself not finishing the bridge versus Jane completing work among friends. The bridge defines me as my father's daughter and helps span the distance between us, but it also makes me want to embrace my daughter's way more tightly.

5

The images I have of Jane's friends are positive and simplified, closely connected to what kind of play emerges between them. That is largely determined by what qualities each brings out in the other or by what the combined qualities of the two bring out: sweetness with Cary; a guarded maturity with Jessica; with Ravenna, a certain proprietary intimacy. As I tend to romanticize their parents, I romanticize the girls, drawing conclusions from the surface of their play that suit myself. But even that limited perspective of social interaction teaches me.

With Cary, Jane often draws and copies. After seeing the movie *Aladdin*, the girls repeatedly copied or drew freehand Princess Jasmine, their make-believe heroine. Then, Jane decided she wanted to buy for Cary the Princess Jasmine doll. As such a present threatened to use up weeks of her allowance, I called Cary's parents. After a quick exchange with Cary, her mother called back. Cary wanted to give Jane the Princess Jasmine doll in exchange for Jane's gift to her.

One night, Jane called Cary, and over the wires the girls drew a matching kitten curled up sleeping. We parents in our separate homes, making supper or washing up, caught snatches of the conversation describing first the animal's ears, then its face, its body, its tail, and its rug, and we watched in passing the skillful drawing evolve under the impetus of a shared interest between friends.

When Jane wants a friend over to play, she most often calls Cary. Once she remarked that both she and Cary had brown hair. As many of her friends have brown hair, she may have meant that only she and Cary live in apartments, have no siblings, and like to do many of the same things. But she does not call Cary her best friend, only one of her best friends.

With Jessica, not Cary, Jane plays dolls. As soon as Jessica arrives with her doll, Jenny, Jane runs to get Baby. While their mothers visit, the two dollies amuse each other, eat meals together, and get frequently changed and dressed. I catch glimpses of this play too, noting how Jessica handles Jenny as if she is alive. While considerate of her baby's imaginary wishes and needs, at the same time she seems to enjoy her. I am surprised and wonder if, away from adult eyes, she includes this sophisticated mothering ability in her role as class leader.

As for Jane, she is playing pretend with her friend Jessica. Baby comes second in importance. Even stuffed animals, Jane's friends and comforters as they were mine, are removed from the level of Jenny's reality. If Jessica is coming over to go to the movies, for instance, rather than to play with Jenny, Jane sometimes checks to make sure Baby has not been left in a state of neglect which might shock her friend.

I do not recall playing with dolls as a child, either by myself or with a friend. But when I was pregnant with Jane, my mother related how she took me as a small child to visit a friend and her toddler. I kept trying to pick the latter up, calling it "Dolly," until my mother had to say good-bye. I cried for Dolly all the way home, while my mother tried to explain that Dolly was a live little boy who did not want to be held by me and taken away.

When inclined, petite, elegant Lila, another best friend of Jane's, expertly acts out the part of a baby, so then Jane has in a way the live dolly I wanted. When Mommy Jane carries her around the apartment, Baby Lila is happy. But when put to bed and left in the dark, she wakes every few seconds and cries. She not only cries but is sick. Her mother does not complain. Cheerfully, she pretends to clean and change her baby with big scarves tied over Lila's blue jeans—all by flashlight.

I was a couple of years older than Jane when I met my best friend. We did not draw together or play dolls or act out Mommy and Baby. Hearing snatches of Jane's and Lila's dialogue, I laugh, as they do themselves. A long forgotten—was it ever realized—sense of fun overtakes me. Whenever I see Lila's serious face, as serious as my own, it emphasizes my inner image of her unlocking a side of myself I did not know existed.

How often do I paint unknown sides of myself, and when I do, how often do I paint over them because I fail to recognize their validity?

6

Last fall, soon after school started, Jane and her classmates were asked to draw themselves. That self-portrait, hanging in her room, smiles at me through a child's draftsmanship. Suddenly wondering how my daughter sees herself, I look at it closely. Pencil contrasts with crayon; hard lines with softer, rounder ones. The smile is red crayon, but its bold line and color follow a slightly ambivalent course. The eyes, drawn in pencil, are different from each other: one piercing and stern, if somewhat anxious, the other wide with pleasure. Drawn sideways in the otherwise frontal view, the nose resembles a lean, upside-down question mark, except for the sudden indentation and skillful curve of the nostril.

After the self-portraits were completed, the children were asked to pick positive adjectives to describe each other's personalities. For Jane they picked "Shy, friendly, nice" but missed one other important, "positive" quality.

Until her fourth birthday Jane did not sleep through the night. Being artists and having only one child, Bob and I could be more flexible than many parents, but the frequent interruption of sleep, three or four times a night, took its toll. Bob did not participate in the rising-at-night routine, although often Jane's cries woke him too, but he took over the shopping, cooking, and most of the outside world's demands which, until then, we had divided between us.

One night early in her second year, we decided to let Jane cry. As advised, we went into her bedroom every little while with longer spaces between each visit, laid her down—she insisted on standing—patted her back, and left. Still she cried. Finally, after staying away an hour, during which her cries increased in desperation and rage, we went in to find her at the crib's railing, hanging from it whenever her feet gave out. I decided then that I could afford to get up with her until the night awakenings ceased. When I asked Bob what he thought, he said grownups could usually find comfort from others or from something when they woke up lonely or frightened, but could babies?

The direction in which we are trying to raise Jane first presented itself then in a definitive way. After that mutual, initial decision, Bob and I attempted to impose less rather than more discipline. If we interfered less with the various stages of early childhood, Jane might learn to think more for herself. A sociable but shy toddler, if her stubbornness was not squelched in the beginning, she might stand up for herself better.

During the weeks immediately following her birth her cry would inevitably permeate my first hour of deep sleep. Then it would repeat itself, gaining in strength. In order to spare the neighbors I would rise too abruptly, cross the hall with my heart pounding, and pick up the baby. After some time her crumpled face would settle into serene lines. I would carefully move to lower her into the crib, but instantly her eyes would fly open and her tiny body convulse with shock. This would happen again and again. My arms would gently hold her while often I silently wept in anger, my interrupted dreams hovering over me. I knew the eventual victory of a sleeping child did not count for much because a few hours later she would begin again. Gradually, over more than a thousand three hundred nights of trying to make her sleep, I was a different person, and so was she.

I will not receive an award for my effort. The world will say I brought it on myself: I should have taken the baby into Bob's and my bed or moved the crib into our room. I should not have come to her so quickly when she cried. I should have emphasized, when she was a little older, that we were across the three-foot-wide hall with our door open; she could call us any time. I should have investigated the building's heating system because the pipes were noisy. I should have fed her differently, exercised her more or less, enforced fewer or more numerous quiet times during the day.

But that era is finished, and no matter how I or the world look at it, we cannot change it, although how we regard it may change. Rising with Jane two or three times a night for four years, did I lay the groundwork for an eventual tyrant or at the least for someone who cannot be by herself? Or did I help make a shy, scared child braver and more loving. Or only myself, or neither of us. The saying is, "Know thyself," not "Change thyself."

Technically, I can change paintings when I wish, but eras pass in paintings too, so beyond a certain point change means starting again. Even that is all right if, when I change work, I know in some way what I am about, even as I knew rising with Jane was what I had to do. Besides, however a painting turns out, most of the present and future world will notice or understand it even less than it does my getting up with my daughter.

The same night that Jane turned four, she slept for six uninterrupted hours and thereafter eight and nine a night, and the memory of our nocturnal hours together faded. If her self-portrait hints at that quality which her classmates neglected to mention, a portrait she drew of me, shortly after drawing herself, proclaims it. My profile slants slightly upwards. So does the gaze of my eye and the corner of my mouth. The latter detail gentles the overall heroic severity of the image. Outsiders have said the drawing does nothing for me, but Jane and I know it is me. But is it? Or does it leave too much out?

7

In the summer following fourth grade I read *Little Women* for the first time, straddled across my bed on my stomach, barely taking time to eat. The story centers around a mother and her four daughters who are growing up in New England during the second half of the nineteenth century. When they are introduced to the reader, the girls are teenagers, except for the youngest, who is ten or eleven. At the story's end they are grown up and married with young children of their own. The author, Louisa May Alcott, reportedly did not enjoy writing the book, although she claimed, "We really lived most of it, and if it succeeds that will be the reason."

At the time of my first reading, I identified most with Beth, the peacemaker: the sweet and more unassertive member of the family. But my heroine was Jo, the character based on Louisa May Alcott herself. Not until I was a teenager did I begin to see signs of Jo in myself. By my early thirties I felt I *was* the grownup Jo, but then Jo's creator's life, as described by her biographers, flashed before me as a warning. Particularly Martha Saxon's 1977 version in *Louisa May, A Modern Biography of Louisa May Alcott*. Saxon contended that not only was Louisa haunted by loneliness the unmarried state tended to bring about in those days, but fulfillment as a writer eluded her, driven as she was to please her family and public. I worried her fate might become my own. At that point I began to question the deeper implications of the mature Jo's self-control and denial. Did those qualities work towards her fulfillment, as the book implies, or did that come to her fortuitously? Was the unhappy life of the author the more realistic outcome of the character that Jo from the beginning is instructed to cultivate?

Although Louisa May Alcott is sympathetic to her heroine's imaginative, stubborn nature, for the most part she backs the outlook of the times and place: Jo *should* shed her tomboy ways and curb her anger even to the point of not feeling it. Such ideals to which the girls were supposed to conform seem somewhat limited today. Did Louisa May Alcott plod through the writing of the book because she consciously or unconsciously objected to those ideals, even as she supported them in her writing?

Or did she plod because writing the book hurt her? She had not "lived most of it." She and her family, as pointed out by Saxton, had complicated natures and family pasts that could not be fitted into a tidy moral picture acceptable to their times. Real fulfillment was out of reach. On the most concrete level, for example, the focus of Louisa May Alcott's adult life as a writer did not allow for the husband, children, and management of a boys' school, including the writing of a good book, all of which is assigned to Jo's future.

In my early thirties I did not question Jo's vision of fulfillment, only whether it was possible for her. Marmee, whose wisdom I admired, seemed less real than her daughters. Was that how Louisa May Alcott, at age thirty-six when she wrote the book, saw her mother? If so, there was the possibility, I thought as I drew nearer to thirty-six, severe and focused myself, that Marmee's self-control and denial resulted in a certain lack of feeling that over the years turned her into the slightly flat, moralistic character who presided over not only the fictitious daughter but the real one. Or, was the idealized portrait of her mother indicative of a more complicated love, inclusive of blame and anger, that Louisa was afraid to disclose?

A few days ago when I was working on my book, Jane asked me to read it to her. I did not object to Bob seeing it, but I was worried about its influence on her.

"I could read some parts to you, but it's really for grown-ups and most likely would bore you. I'm writing about you and Daddy and Homer and Grandma, but above all, I'm writing about myself.

"Your drawing of me on the door tells quite a lot about me, don't you agree, but it tells just as much or more about you.

"I hope you will like my portrait of you as much as I do yours of me, but it can't *be* you any more than your drawing can be me. For one thing, you and I are always changing.

"And how about the people who look at your drawing or read my book? They are each different and have different ideas about what they see or read.

"I am a private person. That's why I am a painter, not a writer, but if the book turns out well, I might try to get it published," I concluded. "The publisher would make a cover and jacket for it and sell it in bookstores."

Earlier in the spring, just after I finished the talk on being an artist, Jane hugged and hugged me. I thought it was because she was proud of me, but it may have been more because she was so glad to have me back from the podium.

When I reread *Little Women* in my early thirties, I reflected upon Jo, as a grown woman, waiting for something or someone to discover her. Around that time, I met Bob at a crowded party. For most of the evening I had been in a different room, unaware of his presence. Then the friend who had persuaded me to come pushed her way over and said, "There's somebody I want you to meet." I followed her into another room, and there was Bob. The couch, on which he was sitting by himself for the moment, was not a podium but seemed exposed. Resolutely, I ignored the surrounding, watching guests, while my shy self stepped forward to meet a stranger, revealing its delight in him for all to see. I moved towards him even as he smiled at me and patted the empty seat beside him.

I remember the anxiety I felt when I looked at Jane's self-portrait. "Why?" I ask myself. Maybe because I have never looked at Jane that way before, as if she were not my perfect, invulnerable heroine. Looking at her drawing of me, I am reminded of Jo's literary sketch of Marmee. Maybe it was time for Jane to regard me as less of an ideal. I would dislike her writing about me the way Louisa May Alcott did her mother. Or maybe I resemble Marmee more than I do Jo or the writer, Louisa May Alcott, who finished many books. And how will I write about my own mother?

Although spurred on in part by the goal of a published book, my writing, if honest, might help my world and me know each other better, for so much privacy in the past has encouraged me to hide not only from myself and the world but from those closest to me.

When I was a young child, sometimes I would lay, holding my breath, on the tropical ocean floor, its soft sand bottom shaped into waves by the water's movement, and I would look up three, four, or five feet through my mask at the surface. On the beach I looked up at a similar surface miles away. The clouds curled and moved like the surface formations seen from underneath the shallower ocean. At the time I believed, if necessary, I could walk as safely and freely on the watery ocean's bottom as I did on the airy one's. My sense of security, whether false or not, comes from feeling I am hidden on a bottom looking up through layers of water, or air, and light rather than exposed on a surface looking down.

8

Once a week I have supper with my mother. Sometimes Bob comes, or Jane, or Bob and Jane, but often I drive out to the retirement community by myself. My mother and I walk or drive to the big dining room and after dinner come back to her house and talk. We discuss certain political goings-on and how work is progressing and what family members are up to, and for a time I have my mother to myself, a rare experience when I was a child.

I once came across a faded photograph of two arms and hands reaching and the blurred face above also reaching towards a small, barefooted figure in a white nightgown. The adult figure, my mother, is leaning towards me, her two- or three-year-old, and her posture expresses love and delight.

One day after school when I was ten, I hugged my mother around her waist from behind while she was doing some work at the sink. She shook me off impatiently. "You're too big to be hanging on me now," she said.

The dependence of a ten-year-old probably felt like a weight to her at the time, dragging her down along with the loneliness and sadness that late winter afternoons in the north sometimes invoke. In my shoes Jane would have said angrily, "Go away. You're nasty." But I left without a word and climbed the stairs to do my homework.

When I was in my late twenties, my mother and I visited my grandparents over a weekend. Watching my mother's devotion to her mother, I became increasingly upset. A couple of years earlier my mother had made an edition of woodcut prints. Afterwards, she had turned the block into a hand-painted, low-relief sculpture and given it to me as a present. But the paint had faded. I had brought the block, along with a brush and more durable paint, from my city apartment for her to retouch. As she hastened on yet another errand for her mother, I stopped her. "You promised to fix the block," I reminded her.

"In a minute," she said, moving on, missing in her haste what I really wanted.

"No, now," I commanded.

My mother stopped to look at me: her grownup, suddenly agonized daughter. "All right," she said. "Where is it?"

9

Six years older than me, my sister Anne was my second mother, less important to me than my real one but in some ways more powerful, especially during my preteen and teenage years, as I tried to explain to Jane. We were on one of our walks with Homer, and she had asked about my sisters.

"How did she control you?"

"Well, she liked me a lot and did many nice things for me, and I liked her. We had special times together. But she expected me to be a certain way, and I went along with her expectations."

"Like Jessica?"

"Exactly like Jessica," I replied, and I thought of that particular friend of Jane's whose wishes were all the harder to resist because of the hurt she sustained whenever they were denied.

"Does Anne still like you?"

"She does. She loves me. But a long time ago before I met Daddy, I got angry at her, and it took her many years to forgive me."

After Bob and I decided to get married, a friend invited us to dinner to celebrate.

"Why," asked my friend's husband, playing the comedian, "do you want to marry this man?"

"Because I can get angry at him," I glibly replied.

Laughter followed my words, but my friend nodded and said, "That's a good reason."

For me to express anger, except to strangers, was rare until

I met Bob and became a mother. I never saw my parents angry at each other, only at us children. But that anger frightened me, as it usually resulted in a spanking. And for one of us to express anger at them, as Jane does almost daily at Bob or me, was unthinkable.

I remember three times getting angry on the spot at somebody I knew, apart from Bob and Jane. When I was younger than Jane, my older brother and I had a fistfight over a toy train set; at Jane's age I fought my grandfather when he took me away from a bullfrog; and in my late twenties I spoke cruelly to Anne. That occurred about the same time as my rebellion against my mother.

Over the years, small, unexpressed hostilities built into something bigger and unsuspected by Anne. Coming from the same family as myself, where anger was seldom voiced and overwhelmed us when it was, she was a bad recipient for my outburst. My instinct not to hurt her, otherwise consistent throughout our relationship, was swayed before and during my outburst by a logic which proclaimed the necessity of a break with her in order to make a life of my own.

Ironically, my desire to protect her had prevented me from speaking up along the way. Like Louisa May Alcott's Beth, for years I had been the peacemaker, even the sacrificial lamb of the family, or so I thought. At the time of my attack on Anne I agreed with a man who insinuated she kept me in that role more than anybody else. I may have misinterpreted him, but whether he was to blame or not, he spurred me on, in love with him as I was. In any case, whether correct or not, my logic was less excusable than Jo's emotional reaction to the immediate wrong done when Amy burned up her story.

My anger, that of a younger sibling against an older, more dominating one, was real enough, but coldly expressed as it was over a minor issue, it devastated Anne more than Jo's did Amy. Breaking out of my family role may have been necessary but not by the means chosen. I can still recall the shock and hurt on Anne's face.

Anger, I have told Jane, can be a way to keep free. It lets others know when they are stepping on your territory in a way that threatens who you are. But it is better to get angry in small doses, as the offenses occur, not in the single, annihilating one I dumped on Anne.

A while after we met and before we lived together and a year or so before we married, Bob and I took a trip to Italy. After years of living alone, we moved steadily but cautiously towards a different state. Sometimes anxious in the face of that transition, it seemed fitting to be physically in a foreign country. Words, always important to me, were without value there, as I did not speak the language. My quiet looks and manners seemed to pass unnoticed. Each night we moved on to another place, so my rooted nature could not grasp hold. While my invisibility made me uncomfortable at times, it freed me too and in some ways enhanced the beauties of the trip. Besides, I was more interested in the internal adventures offered, like getting to know Bob on a daily basis instead of how we had known each other before: a special day together interspersed with a few reflective days apart.

I remember one small town in particular, or rather a night when the rain fell on the cobbled stones and splashed against the dark window of a restaurant. We were looking in, reading the posted menu by lamplight. Bob was amused by some of the translations into English of the fare. The next morning I opened my eyes under a large, foreign, hotel window, an ocher green light from the trees outside flooding the room. I woke with a feeling of joy caused by this dream.

I was to play an important tennis match, but at the last moment discovered that my racket had gaps in its strings, so I ran to borrow Anne's. I jumped from plastic sheets covering plants as tall as buildings onto lower sheets and smaller plants and landed running. Bob, at my side, seemed unaware that I was racing to make a deadline. He kept talking about something else. I ran on, sure I would lose him. We passed a baby in its carriage, and a dog who barked at us. When we fell, we bounced back high into the air. Then we were running to return the racket to Anne in time for her own game. She was waiting racket-less on an empty court. Then I woke up.

I told the dream to Bob and mentioned it again that night when we were exploring Assisi's dark and quiet streets. Unfriendly all of a sudden, he remarked that he had not listened to it earlier. We walked along in silence. Then he said, "Tell me about it now."

Our giddy run together, the baby carriage and the dog and, most of all, Bob's staying with me—running to meet his own deadline, perhaps, but staying with me—was the principal cause of my elation, which I failed to explain to him.

Bob does not think of himself as a joyous person, and possibly my joy that day made him feel a lack, so he turned on me. Recently, he had a show, and a viewer remarked to me that the paintings seemed full of joy.

"Your comment would surprise my husband," I said, surprised myself. But as I looked around at the work, I could see what she meant.

"Does Anne forgive you now?" Jane asked during our walk.

"She does," I said. But I sighed.

Sometimes I think of the dream and its joy. That it included Anne makes me wonder. Did my anger at her and her subsequent emotional break from me have something to do with my finding Bob and eventually Jane? What did I say to her then? Was it something like, "You're not being kind. You think you are, but you're just trying to control me. Back off. Leave me alone?"

In my dream I ran towards her with no fear of being controlled or desire to control, only with the urgency of a debt to pay. Even as she had let go and given me my freedom, I wanted her to be free.

Six years later, when Jane is in eighth grade, Anne sits opposite me across a decorated table. She is giving a birthday luncheon for my mother. She mentions that her husband has secured a place for her to write over the summer. She is excited, having been trying to complete a novel for years. A cousin impatiently claims that she is deceiving herself and will never finish.

Anne replies that the remark is not encouraging: what she needs is support. Later, when saying good-bye, she embraces her.

When Jane is in the third grade, Bob says nothing about a painting I bring from my studio, hang on a wall, and declare finished.

"Why don't you comment anymore when I come home with a painting that's finally done?"

"Because I know it isn't. Why should I waste my time commenting when I know the next day it will disappear and come back totally changed?"

"Well, it's not that often I think a painting is completed, certainly less often than you, and I comment on your work."

"Because when I say a painting's finished, it's finished. My paintings are not endless movies."

"That's how I paint. When I am really through, what I have completed seems perfect to me."

"It does?" Bob sounds skeptical. "You're a fortunate painter."

"Yes," I agree. "Maybe I have a beam in my eye, but it seems perfect to me, even over time. You finish more good paintings than I do, but not so many more."

"Are you belittling my work?"

"No, and I know you don't mean to belittle mine when you don't comment on it.

"Besides, if you look at it another way, your paintings disappear almost as quickly as mine."

"What do you mean?"

"Because they sell."

"I work at it."

Our conversation is like a painting I must resolve, right away. Take out this word; put in that one; switch these sentences to the beginning; those to the middle or end. Make peace. But now the painting is muddied and lost.

I hesitate, then let the conversation stand.

10

For two summers, when I was fifteen and sixteen, Anne invited me to her house in Canada and with her husband financed flying lessons for me. During that time she had a photograph of me on her bureau.

Towards the end of the second summer she found a letter I had written but not mailed. Its dramatic recording of events cast an unfavorable light on her way of life and on a couple of her companions. I had carelessly slipped it inside the bottom of the pad before starting again. Instead of instructing me against a basic social liability, the incident made me connect writing with inflicting pain.

Shortly after Anne discovered the letter, I received my pilot's license. Although I had logged the required hours of solo flight, for a brief time during the cross-country section of the exam I had become lost. For all my height, western Canada had stretched indecipherable below me. Static on the radio made it inaccessible and compounded my confusion and alarm.

A few days earlier my instructor had flown me over an isolated field, framed by telephone wires, and demonstrated what I was to do for the emergency landing maneuver: fly low, look the field over for rocks and other impediments, gain altitude again, cut the motor, glide down, touch the wheels to the ground, give full throttle, and lift the nose so steeply I was sure we would stall. Bad weather and my departure date eliminated the extra days I needed to practice the drill, first with him, then on my own. During the exam, just before getting lost, I found the field, circled it, and left without making an approach.

I realized the significance of obtaining a pilot's license only after I returned home and felt the world's respect for it. At the time it was Anne's unquestioning attitude that led me to the test; our parents' caution over their first child, which had denied her such documented adventure at my age, may have influenced her.

I volunteered no information about getting lost or the aborted touch-and-go. Whether my instructor knew or not, he questioned Anne closely as to whether I intended to fly on my own in the future. Once assured of my lack of interest along those lines, he granted me my imperfect finish. As generous and beneficial to my confidence and welfare as Anne's support was, it was part of her vision, never examined by me.

Nor did I question driving to and from the airport. Almost as new to the art of driving as flying, I had to navigate an elevated, winding highway with speeding trucks and cars mostly far bigger than my assigned, noisy common gear.

What I cared about at the time was the instructor and his proximity in the small plane's cabin. When I began my solo flights, I remember my sense of loss rather than the excitement of doing something I liked on my own.

So, I was less different from others than I have supposed. Even the summer I passed by myself on Lupin was less the choice of an isolationist than of a woman hoping, through nature and time to herself, to resolve an unhappy relationship.

I regard my pilot log book and its neatly recorded hours of solo flight with the same element of disbelief as I do the distances I rowed each day during that summer. I see a young woman hastening up the hill from the cookhouse to the deserted main house in order to get to bed before dark, then lying awake for a long time while owls hooted and floors creaked.

Anne had her husband, a lifestyle she had dreamt of, plans for children of her own. Did envy have anything to do with the letter I wrote but did not send? Did Anne's—in some ways—restricting vision of me as a pilot flying high and free, or of an artist, stem from what she had chosen not to do and be at that time?

11

When I was in fifth grade, Lisa, a classmate of mine, tried for a while to usurp my best friend. "Who's your best friend, Kate or me?" she asked during the one time I played at her house. I was sitting on the floor while she, lit up by gray, late afternoon rays from a window at my back, was enthroned in an armchair opposite me. "Say I'm your best friend," she urged. When I finally complied, the victory in her smile made me feel small.

My mother sensed something about Lisa and, thereafter, supported by my father, refused to let me play with her outside of school. Such an overt act of control and interference from her towards her fourth child was the first and last of its kind. It stood by itself, and even at the time I respected it, despite my outrage.

Since then, I have talked to Lisa on the phone and heard the distant voice and laugh of a friend who tracked down for me the telephone number of another classmate.

At Jane's age I had sisters and brothers and cousins but not friends. Occasionally, a child my age would come to the island for a short time and then go away again. Nursery school and first grade were up north, each in a different place; second grade on the island; third grade skipped. When I began fourth grade in a northern school I was to attend for the next six years, I met Kate.

I do not remember what or how we played together, but at least one image comes to mind suggestive of our, at times, rather complex behavior. Early on in our relationship, maybe reasoning that in the long run it was the kindest way, Kate and I told a third friend that we no longer wanted to be best friends with her. We watched her break down in front of us. "I believe that was my own inspired idea," Kate wryly informed me almost four decades later.

Although Jane and her friends are only in second grade and we were in fourth, some of the same issues such as competition between friends and leaving a friend out have already surfaced in Jane's world. But Kate and I did not have teachers who watched over our social behavior.

"I worry about interfering too much," I told Jane's first grade teacher. "I want Jane to learn to work things out for herself."

"Worry about not interfering enough," she replied. "Parents often don't realize that children need as much guidance socially as academically."

Other than in fourth grade, when I met her, and in ninth grade, when girls and boys were separated, Kate and I were not in the same section, and I do not recall feelings of competition between us. But I suspect that they existed and that my lapse of memory in this respect stems from my refusal at the time to acknowledge them.

Kate, who excelled in academics and sports, was a popular leader, and her immediate acceptance of me and her subsequent loyalty protected me. My school image, colored by hers of me, was true to myself in large part but not completely. At times it was constraining, as was Kate. Even if not on her level, I was good enough at academics and sports, and at the time I seemed more artistic. But the balance of power between us tipped in her direction, although not to the degree it had with Lisa.

During fourth grade and the years that followed, Kate remained my best friend, and, while I was with her, the authoritarian side of my own nature was rarely visible to me or others. Now I recall a friend and I riding our bikes somewhere outside of town during summer vacation on Flamingo. Her father, a minister, worked briefly on the island and then departed, taking his family with him. The conversation we had along the way escapes me, but not my feeling of control and the barely hidden resentment on my friend's face.

After a class reunion luncheon eight and a half years ago, the headmaster wanted to take us on a tour of the school. The group wavered. I eventually assented, while Kate refused and stayed behind with a following. Looking back at that moment, I see myself, under the spell of my past school image, quickly suppressing a feeling of competition with my best friend.

In my late twenties and early thirties I had trouble sleeping. Eventually, I consulted a doctor recommended by a friend. For an hour a week over the course of a year he sat in a chair opposite mine, his casual male presence teaching me something my father's might have had he lived and been available. When my doctor had a cold, he would blow his nose without self-consciousness and toss the tissues carelessly into the wastepaper basket.

Once, when I misunderstood a scheduling and failed to show up, the following session he greeted me with barely contained anger and accused me of intentionally skipping out. I surprised us both by saying mildly, "Originally, you asked me to trust you, so it's only fair you trust me."

With the exception of that declaration, what he said, brief and infrequent as it was, interested me more than what I had to say. While touching on an evening I had just passed with the friend who had recommended him and her husband, I admitted to being careful about my clothes and speech. I did not want to outshine her.

"Do you just assume you could?" he asked with a laugh. "That's not giving either of them enough credit."

12

Competition between Jane and Jessica existed from the beginning in kindergarten, but Jane did not acknowledge it. When Jessica wanted something, Jane and the other girls would try to get it for her.

"Jane, is this really necessary?" I would ask, watching her go to such lengths to satisfy what seemed to me a whim of Jessica's.

"Of course, Mom," she would reply indignantly, "Jessica wants it."

If a friend, Jane for instance, played too much with another friend, a wave of hurt would pass over Jessica's face. She would refuse to talk to Jane for the rest of the school day. But last fall when this happened, Jane began to ask her teacher if she and Jessica could be excused to talk in the hall. "Jessica and I need to talk," she would say.

The competitiveness between the two girls remains academic as well as social. When Jane saw her fall report card which, unlike her first grade report card, had grades as well as comments, a couple of S pluses alongside the G's upset her. Then she discovered Jessica had received all G's, including one in art.

"Jessica is Jessica," I said to Jane. "You are you." Jane's reaction to Jessica's grades surprised me. Jane was my heroine, and her relationships with her friends were magical, proof of her social wisdom. In part, I wanted her to work things out for herself because I believed she knew best. Because of my inability to cope with it, I had denied my competitiveness with Kate. Now I denied Jane's with Jessica for much the same reason and told myself it all stemmed from Jessica. There had been a highly visible sign to the contrary.

About a month into second grade, Jane, by means of the inventive spelling encouraged in the classroom, wrote the following about a canoe trip she had just taken with Bob and me, another couple, and their seven-year-old daughter:

> I Wnt Don a Rivr in a Knoo and I Sa (saw) aMaGRT (muskrat) and a TRDL (turtle) and a HaRing (heron) and Than We STOP IN The sand for aPicknik. aFDRWRS WE FAD (fed) The Dacs in the PanD and We last (lost) a Toy Pape (puppy) in the WoDR (water). Than on the wa Hom (home) I Gat a BaBy Pamkin (pumpkin). Im goin to Prt (put) a Bab (bad) Fas no (on) it. it was a Grat Day it was so Grat I Fal aslep in The car. I Dibit (didn't) fanD (find) the Pape (puppy). I Dont no war the Cnoo chrip was.

Shortly thereafter, Jessica wrote a poem which was published in the school newsletter. The spelling was almost perfect, the rhymes excellent, the content spirited, like Jessica herself, and openly competitive, the young heroine outdoing her older sister. Seeing the newsletter on my desk, Jane angrily crumpled it and threw it on the floor.

Her next report card contained all G's, but by then the shock of grades had lessened, and her teacher had taken in the social situation. Although she favored Jessica, which Jane realized early on, she tried to be fair. She moved the two girls' desks apart and watched over them. Under her guidance they learned to work things out. They took different after-school classes and had other best friends over to play and spend the night, as well as each other. Then, ice skating, an outside school activity and mutual interest, threw them competitively together, away from their teacher's eye.

During first grade Jane had met Ravenna, who attended a different school but was present Monday nights at the ice skating class. Those nights were special to Jane because of Ravenna, her special friend, and because the two of them were learning something special in a place away from everyday school. Ravenna's mother, Bob, or I—usually it was I because I enjoyed it more than the other two did—would drive the girls over to the rink, watch them skate for an hour, and drive them home. But in the winter of second grade Jessica decided to take ice skating lessons too, and her parents signed her up for the beginners' class. Jane was unhappy. "It's Ravenna's and my special time," she said. "I look forward to it all week."

Unlike Jane, I welcomed Jessica's arrival. I looked forward to sitting on the bleachers with her mother or father and watching the children skate while we discussed parental concerns.

On the drive over to the rink for the first winter session I heard Jane and Ravenna hinting their intention to exclude Jessica. "I think it would be mean to leave Jessica out," I said tentatively. "Why not make a play date just between yourselves on Saturday?"

But Jessica's mother refused to have her daughter snubbed, and after observing the rather oblique welcome the latter received, spoke to me. Whereupon, I drew Jane aside and said she must include Jessica on Monday nights.

Despite Jane's misgivings, the first eight weeks of lessons passed uneventfully. Jessica had class when Jane and Ravenna had practice and practice when they had class. Then she was promoted, and her new class was at the same time as Jane's and Ravenna's. They no longer had their practice time to themselves and claimed Jessica would not let them work. Jessica's mother and I advised them to teach Jessica, who then said their tricks were too hard. She wanted them to follow her and do her tricks. Well then, how about letting Ravenna and Jane work with each other for half the practice time? The three could skate together the remaining half. One Monday night Ravenna brought a best friend from her school to skate with them during practice. The other two liked her. Suddenly, for no reason we parents could see, it was working out. Jessica and Ravenna became friendly. Jane might have felt left out at times, but she did not seem to mind. When Jessica decided not to enroll again, Jane was sad. When she saw Jessica and her mother unexpectedly back at the rink the beginning of spring session, her face lit up. And the bad memories Jessica's mother and I had of leaving other children out or of being left out were softened by the final harmony between the girls and by our part in encouraging it.

I begin to see that more control, rather than less, is sometimes needed from me as a parent. While it was Ravenna's and Jane's intent to exclude Jessica that provoked my initial, spoken interference, it was Jessica's mother who helped force through this particular rebirth of mine, enabling me to act for the first time upon Jane's first grade teacher's advice.

Jessica had assumed Ravenna had become Jane's very best friend, but when I made the same assumption in a passing remark, Jane instantly corrected me. I suppose Jessica and I had confused special with best. Later this spring, when Ravenna's parents transferred Ravenna to Jane's school, she was no longer a special friend but a best friend Jane had to share with her other best friends.

As for Jessica and Jane, close as they are to each other in certain respects, as yet they do not relax together for long periods of time. The issues of control and competition hang in the air between them, eventually exhausting them. But is my assessment of their relationship correct, or do such issues in my own relationships color my observations too intensely?

Last summer Kate informed me she was writing a book in her spare time. Six or seven months later, I started to write, something Bob had suggested I do over a year ago. "Make some money," he had half joked. But suggestion by itself was not enough to make me listen.

13

On the first day of second grade, while walking Homer with me after school, Jane informed me that everybody in the class could read except her.

Thinking this over, I had to admit to myself that I read so much to her for my own pleasure and education and hers that I neglected getting her to read to me. I could not recall a single attempt in the past three months. As always, over the summer, I had read to her both in Maine and at home: in Maine during those often hot, still afternoons while we lay in the hammock on the porch overlooking the sea; in the city, after she came home from day camp, sitting on the big bed in the cooler bedroom with pillows behind our backs.

"Well," I said in a brisk voice, "we'll start tonight. Read to me ten minutes every night, and you'll soon be a good reader.

"Besides," I added, looking up at the leaves, green but getting drier and skinnier before changing color, "we read together a lot this summer, and I think understanding is the most important thing."

From the start I have read to Jane, and the books I read have absorbed us equally. Especially during our earlier years together, sleep-deprived and Jane-orientated as I was, my mind could not grasp the adult literature I was accustomed to before her birth. So it began to regrow with her books. In the beginning we looked at simple picture books together. *Pat the Cat* series were soon worn and falling apart. A little later, the fish that did not have any fur or feet and swam

around under the river in the *Little Fur Family* filled us both with wonder. So it went until the more mature readings of the present and recent past.

All these books offered us both a social education; I chose them with that main purpose in mind. But the ears with which we listen to stories are mysterious, trained or untrained. What Jane learns from our reading is beyond my control and may surprise me. It already has. The answer to something I have puzzled over has come to mind. Where did Kindergarten Jane get the idea of making a butter churn? From our reading together over a previous summer Laura Ingalls Wilder's *Little House in the Big Woods*.

Strangely enough, having reaped less attention in art than in writing at school, the former is what I decided to concentrate on, and during the last three years of college I took only required English courses. Recalling the special literature and writing classes I missed, I see my college self as a deep sea creature on an ocean floor hemmed in by a constricted, watery view while far above me the surface sparkled with options I never noticed or considered.

Two incidents, either one of which might have made me surface and take measure, failed to budge me. While working on a college still life assignment, I happened to observe the canvas of the only other student—someone I did not know —in the studio at that hour. She was using a thick brush and painting with what I saw as complete freedom and assurance. Her image, a vase with flowers, went so far beyond itself I was stunned. We were the last ones to the dining room for lunch, and I looked wonderingly at her across the empty tables.

The other incident involved my English professor. When I came to his office to ask him for a recommendation to graduate art school, he looked at me surprised and said with a shrug, "I presumed you were going into literature."

In the spring of Jane's eighth grade year I heard on the radio the quote by Red Smith: "There is nothing to writing. All you have to do is sit down at the keyboard and open up a vein." A month or so later Kurt Vonnegut stated in *The New York Times:* "... here is what I tried to get away with [as a writing teacher], only in effect, not actually: I asked each student to open his or her mouth as wide as possible. I reached in with a thumb and forefinger to a point directly beneath his or her epiglottis. There is the free end of a spool of tape there.

"I pinched it, then pulled it out gradually, gently, so as not to make the student gag. When I got several feet of it out where we could see it, the student and I read what was written there."

Perhaps fear of writing's loneliness bothered me less twenty-nine years ago than the unacknowledged possibility of bleeding to death or gagging.

Now is another time, and I am writing to help untangle trouble in the profession I chose years ago. With my mind regrown by Jane's books, I see that from the beginning literature has interested me primarily on account of its characters and their relationships to each other; just as where and how I place the objects in my still lifes is of first importance. Although my reading and writing have been mostly solitary acts, the end has always been social enlightenment. Thus, becoming more social may not be a matter of changing so much as looking differently at what I am and at what reading and writing and painting are to me: ultimately social acts.

But now is another time. Back then, was that college student really unaware of her options, or did she sense them like live things, their tops floating far above, sparkling in the sun, but with tentacles hanging down within easy reach? Did she somehow know—innocent as she was of Smith's and Vonnegut's warnings—that if she entangled herself in them at that time, they might have stopped her breathing?

14

The place I like best to read aloud to Jane is in the hammock which swings on the porch of our summer house and overlooks the sea. Most of the year Bob, Jane, Homer, and I live in our city apartment. But for part of the summer we go to Lupin, the island in Maine where my father spent much of his childhood and which we own with my mother, my siblings, their families, and family on my father's side. For three weeks, the place is ours, although at another time in the summer we come back and share it with extended family. The big, wooden main house, its design first sketched by my grandmother, reminds me of a swallow, osprey, or eagle with its peaked, two-storied center and pair of ground-level wings. It and its surroundings bespeak not only power and wealth belonging to a past that no longer exists for us, but also a sensibility to art, in the form of architecture, and to nature.

For thirty years, with the exception of the summer when my mother came with her children and three nieces and put her back out scything the overgrown grasses of former lawns, Lupin remained closed, unvisited by us or my father's two brothers and their families. The caretaker, who had worked for my grandparents as a young man, lived in the cookhouse with his wife, and they watched over the grounds and buildings, dusting and cleaning the main house once a week and shaking out the sheets that protected the furniture from the sun. When my father in middle age brought his family down for a few days, the caretaker was an old man, and his wife had recently died.

My third visit occurred when I was a year out of college. I spent the summer rising at dawn, drawing, rowing, eating supper with the caretaker in the cookhouse when he was there, going to bed at dusk, and bolting the bedroom door against ghosts. Towards the end of the summer my mother and later an aunt and uncle visited me for a few days, and thereafter during the warmer months of the year various family members began to use the place. After a spell, as some moved away from the east or their children grew older, they came less often, and others took their place.

In the city Bob dreams of Lupin's beauty and spaciousness, especially during the winter months. When the windows are closed against the cold, further shrinking his living and working space, he often concentrates on landscapes he began the previous summer. These paintings hang in our place, enriching and enlarging it, making their subject matter part of home. Sometimes I think that is what the Maine house and island are to Bob more than the condominium apartment.

For Jane and me, the condominium apartment is home. As much as we look forward to Lupin and enjoy it, unlike Bob, we are jubilant upon our return to the city. Our dwelling holds no past history that I know of but our own, and I am freer. I am freer in other respects too. Without school or camp, the demands of painting or writing on Lupin vie daily with those of childcare. The weekend presence of friends balances the island's isolation but exacts its own toll. Once home, I return with relief to my less complicated city routine. Happy to see her room and have television available, Jane looks forward to camp and friends.

But for three weeks a year she can run outside when she wishes. She can climb on the rocks and collect shells and rocks and sea glass from the beaches. As she gets older, she can explore the island and the chilly waters around it by herself or with a cousin or friend or group of friends.

Lupin resonates not only with my father's characteristics but those of his extended family, far back to his Swedish ancestors where in my head grown Ingmar Bergman males dominate: heavy, silent, and unhappy ghosts against whom I locked my bedroom door. In one brown-toned photograph my father stands as a small boy on Lupin ground with his hands together as if in the act of clapping. His head is back, and he is laughing with joy. I never saw him joyful. On the contrary, when we returned to Lupin for that visit, which turned out to be his last before his death a few years later, he read us a short story about a man who failed, and several times his voice broke.

Before we leave Lupin Bob and I tidy and sweep out the house. Once or twice its embrace has caught me by surprise: the golden wood of the inside walls and ceilings and the multi-colored island stones of the fireplaces. For a moment things like the dust that should be removed from the higher beams circling around the tops of the rooms and the horse-hair mattresses that should be replaced are less offensive, and our city place seems small, without history, and too bright.

But even Lupin's embraces, indoors and out, tend to hurt. Beyond family history the answer may lie in one poet's excuse: residing in cities is preferable because the country exposes mortality. Whatever its cause, the emotion Lupin evokes has played a major part in my creative life: landscapes and interiors during earlier years of printmaking, drawing, and watercolor. Could the island influence the still lifes more directly than it has over the past seventeen years? And, more significantly, what effect has my growing tendency to avoid Lupin's kind of pain in the other areas of my life had on finishing work?

15

After my father won the support of the local government, he rented a large section of land on the tropical island of Flamingo for the purpose of making salt. Although he started the business project on his own, he eventually persuaded his two brothers to join him. The property lay outside of town and was covered with deserted pans which were soon fixed up: flat-bottomed, shallow rectangles cut out of the ground and lined with crushed rocks. These were filled with sea water which evaporated, leaving salt. The salt was harvested and conveyored to a central spot until its bases overlapped each other and its peaks rose like those of a stylized, snow-covered mountain range. Periodically, trucks carried loads of it into town to a single, ongoing pile. A ship would appear on the horizon, anchor some distance from shore, take it on from the barges, and leave for a northern destination.

Since the town pile was across the street from our house, my early childhood was full of the sound of trucks and machinery, day and night when a ship was in. So, isolated as island life was, we children felt part of something bigger, as did the adults.

I first left the island to attend nursery school and first grade up north. Then, I returned for second grade during which my mother and a hired tutor instructed me. I skipped third grade. From fourth grade on I went to school up north, but each summer I came back to Flamingo until I was thirteen, when the company was sold, the lease for the land turned over, and my family left for good.

When Jane asked me if I had any friends on Flamingo, I told her that we and the local children were not encouraged to play with each other and that age-wise I did not really fit into any particular grouping of siblings and cousins. But it did not matter, I tried to explain to a child who could not imagine life without friends; there was always the island and things to do with everyone or by one's self.

"Like what?"

"Like swimming once a day. We always looked forward to that. Also, we bicycled and climbed trees or read. Sometimes on the weekend our fathers piled everyone into a truck and took us to a distant beach for a picnic. A great treat was to ride on their shoulders and try to topple each other into the water."

"What did you do by yourself besides read?"

"Well, outside our house there was a ginep tree standing in this very fine sand, typical of where we lived next to passing trucks and wind off the ocean. I liked to play in it with my china animals, moving them around between the tree's roots, making homes for them and imagining their visits and adventures together."

I must have picked quiet times to play there because I don't remember other children around, only the large, hot, deserted yard and the leaves and branches motionless above, protecting me from the sun. Or maybe the yard wasn't deserted, and the trade winds blew as usual, and only my imagination enclosed me in that special, still niche of my own.

"Did you *have* to do anything?"

"Sometimes. Grandma liked to take the girls, my sisters and cousins and me, to sketch and do watercolors outside. There were many things to work from: trees, houses, donkeys, the sea, trucks. The others would each find a spot and get started. By the end of the allotted time, everyone had a complete or nearly complete painting, or so I recall, except me. I would stare at my paper. Draw something. Erase it. Paint in something. Scrub it out."

I paused to think about those expeditions. Before they started, when I was younger, I made some drawings on my own: a child riding a donkey, for example, or two winged horses with their foal. My mother carefully saved such output and gave it to me recently. I looked at it, impressed.

What has happened since then? Over my years as an artist I have completed some things that I like to this day, but long, unproductive periods have plagued my working life, and much of my output lacks what those early drawings have.

I turned back to Jane, discouraged. "Funny I grew up and became an artist. I sometimes wonder why."

Sitting here at my desk, I recall Arthur Miller, the playwright, saying in a television interview that anything valid he had completed had some connection with his childhood. It had just been a matter of finding it.

Once, during a difficult annual meeting on Lupin, a favorite uncle turned on me. Sitting on the porch as we were, I glanced outward, away from the family faces, at the sunny surroundings and saw what I had lost to ugliness: the grounds, the Cook House and Little Boat House down the hill, and the sea.

When Homer got an infection in his head, the first sign of his discomfort was to sit down on a walk and raise a paw. There, I looked in vain for a thorn or sharp stone. Regarding my childhood, Flamingo is the paw, although the location of transferred love rather than pain, while the love for people closest to me lies so dense and deep within my head that, if ever needed, antibiotics could not reach it.

As early as nursery school, I was introduced to my mother's childhood places: the house in the city where she and I lived, I for one school year, she for all the school days until grown; the weekend mountain house where Thanksgivings were held; and the log cabin on the family complex where I stayed for a month during one summer.

Yet, because I lived with my father's side of the family, I was more comfortable in his places—even Flamingo seemed more his in some ways, although it also belonged to my mother. But then, places were not necessary to know her.

My father's two islands help connect my past and present, offering possibilities regarding my work that could validate Arthur Miller's statement. But my mother's places might signify similar, important connections that I have as yet refused to recognize.

16

While each of my parents claimed Flamingo in his or her own way, my mother was never drawn to Lupin nor my father to her family mountain. Each seemed lonely and diminished in those strongholds of the other's past. Early on in their marriage my mother relinquished her shares in her own family's summer complex in Maine. After my father died and we children began to congregate for short periods of time on Lupin, often with our cousins and aunts and uncles, she came infrequently to see us there. Again, she was sharing an island with in-laws rather than siblings, but Lupin's buildings and topography served to make her homesick for the log cabin house she had slept in as a child. She missed the sounds of small creatures sheltered in the moss that grew between the fitted logs. They had comforted her and put her to sleep.

It is true that growing up in my father's places, or in places where his taste or his family's dominated, we children in those ways did not know our mother—primary parent as she was—as well as we knew him. But in the houses my mother occupied after his death she gradually began to make her own taste known, even the one halfway up the mountain which still had many of my father's things. After her parents died, she stayed for a few more years until osteoporosis broke her back. When she began to regain strength and mobility, just after Jane started second grade, she sold her house, divided most of its contents between her five children, and moved to a retirement community twenty minutes from us. Her new house, smaller than our condominium apartment, is her own and inclusive of her life both with and without my father. Its windows look out on woods and a small meadow, a miniaturized childhood view.

Its opposite ends connect with two other houses which were each inhabited by a stranger when she moved in. After a while, their names and those of others began to appear in her conversation. As I listened, I was less startled by this occurrence than by my mother's understanding of each name's possessor. Was her past, relative isolation during the years I had known her due more to priorities and circumstances than to her nature? Or, just as osteoporosis motivated her move to the retirement community, had it also motivated her sociability, surprising her as much as me?

But even her friends, as important as they are to her, do not ultimately dominate her time. For my mother has always had an intense urge to create, particularly in the visual arts and writing. Through the years she has produced a large and varied body of work, much of it given away or sold. Her work and life jump from here to there while mine are more limited and concentrated. But my mother, especially at this time in her life, and I are equally driven each day to seek out the isolation necessary for our work and then to fight against the loneliness we have brought upon ourselves.

Recently, my mother and her two sisters wrote books about their childhood. Nannies and horses are mentioned with attachment, but isolation pervades the background. While growing up, the children moved between the mountain weekend house to the one in New York City during the school week to the less formal, summer complex in Maine. There is a distance between them and between their parents and themselves that the size and number of their houses and frequent packing and unpacking may have encouraged.

My father grew up moving between a big house in a New England town and the one on Lupin, where he spent half the year. He had tutors until he was a teenager, and only then did he attend school with other children. So there is a history of isolation on both sides of the family: one grandfather sought out a mountain as a principal residence, the other an island. After college my father found his own island. His oldest daughter, my sister Anne, was also a teenager when she left it to attend school with children other than her siblings and cousins. Coincidentally or not, when my father and mother decided to leave Flamingo after twenty-five years, Anne, a college freshman, became engaged to a man who lived in the north but had roots on islands relatively near ours. Over the years she has continued to pack and unpack between a spacious, northern house and two small houseboats moored during the winter in remote, tropical waters.

My mother and her sisters write of their childhood as a special time without denying its isolation. Their books open my eyes to my own separateness as a child and the distance that existed between my parents and me and between us siblings while we were growing up. Do large houses and moving back and forth between them make for those distances? Does the small condominium apartment which is Jane's home, except for three or four weeks each summer, lessen them?

It lessens them for me. Our space is the kind I need: small, open, and connected. Grass and trees, not our own, grow outside our windows, and cars pass by the front and back of our building. Above, below, and opposite us, we hear occasional noises from our neighbors. I find comfort in our place, situated as it is amid the moderate sounds and traffic of humans.

Does Jane? I think she does, but she may not stamp her feet and slam her door and bounce hard balls on the floor except this month when the apartment below is for sale and vacant. Nor may she run outside when she wishes, or bicycle all day, or climb ginep trees. The physical freedoms my siblings and I had as children are not available to her.

At its end our hall connects the two bedrooms, one slightly before the other, but at an early age Jane shut her door and put a sign on it which read, "Pease Nok Befor you cum in." Natural enough as her behavior was, it serves to remind me that big houses alone may not cause the deep, if muted, desire for isolation and privacy that seems to mark both sides of my family. It may stem from an inherited nature already passed on to Jane, as yet barely visible beneath her sociability, from Bob's side of the family as well as mine. For, like my father, Bob is sociably inclined on the surface but on a deeper level more alone.

17

Unlike myself at her age, Jane has many friends culled from school, preschool, the children of Bob's and my friends, and one from a family who lived next to my mother on the mountainside. All these friends of Jane's reassure me because I was shy as a child. Although I was too willful to become a victim, the walls that shyness sometimes built around me made me pay attention to Jane's first teacher's words.

"Jane is shy," she said of her one and a half-year-old pupil a week after Jane began attending preschool for three, then four, hours a morning. "She must learn to use her words, or she might become a victim."

Since Jane's preschool concentrated on teaching its children social skills, and her kindergarten through second grade teachers placed as much emphasis on the social curriculum as the academic, I felt relieved of that responsibility. Between Jane's apparent sociability and my lack of it and her school's emphasis upon it, I believed I had little to teach along those lines except the most obvious things. Instead, Jane and her friends taught me.

After Jane started preschool and then kindergarten, I discovered the parents of her friends, and they have also taught me. As I have watched over their children, they have watched over Jane, and together we have formed a ring of support. It has been strengthened at drop-off and pick-up times and brief phone calls concerning the children's school business and holiday plans. Play dates and sleepovers have given us a chance to know our own child and our child's friends better or to rest in our child's absence.

Yet outside our connecting interest we do not know anything more now than in the beginning about what goes on
in each other's heads. We may fear that if we did, conflicts
would threaten to break what we need more than intimacy.
So far, it has been enough to sense supporting, instructive
presences around us and our children. That awareness has
given us courage and assisted at various, personal rebirths
inspired by the children.

This manuscript is a child too. Already I see it cannot be
myself, only my child. And even as I am giving birth to it,
it would not exist without those I am depicting. Seen
through my eyes the latter are the parents of their own
written images: the created Jane, Bob, myself, my mother,
father, Jane's friends, their parents, Homer, whoever might
appear. In order to finish what I have started, I will need
the support and at times guidance of all.

18

For the past nine or ten months have come dreams at night. During the day my mind struggles to retain their imagery, for it is stunning, and the threat implicit in most of it does not alarm me. These dreams are my watchdogs and friends, revealing me to myself. Their stark, threatening beauty balances my everyday life. Usually, no matter how hard I try, even if I write them down, the life of them fades after a few days the same way the color of the seashells in my studio eventually does. Then all I can recall are the outlines.

During my single adult years when my isolation far outweighed my sociability, I had similar dreams of lonely beauty, but the loneliness overwhelmed the beauty, and the dreams were more like nightmares. In one I was the only person alive, and the landscape, as beautiful as it was, offered no hope. So I began to change my ways. I started by saying hello to more people in order that I might sleep, have dreams instead of nightmares, and make art during the workday.

19

During those more solitary years I used to watch a group of elderly neighbors put their chairs on the grassy median between two lanes of moving traffic, though a large and suitable park was just across the drive. They sat in their seats close together, a community, while their thin, green, open car moved along with the others.

I both seek out and struggle against isolation on a daily basis, but I never consider what might be its final form. Bob says not a day goes by without death passing through his thoughts, even before his parents died. Aware of being overweight and constantly under stress, my younger brother, Eddie, once looked at me strangely and remarked, "You think you're going to live forever."

My mother knows she is not. In her new home, death or approaching death is all around her. Right now, she is visiting a friend who has six weeks to live. The friend's daughter spends her time with her mother and strives to encourage her appetite with her cooking skills. On her most recent visit, my mother was offered a cup of the daughter's soup. She said it tasted like ambrosia.

Sometimes she shows me where her latest work is, just in case something happens to her. Her work helps her fight her fear of death, as this book might help me approach mine.

Living in her small space, the larger houses of her past gone and not regretted, and surrounded by people, some of whom she turns to gratefully as friends, my mother seeks out more than ever the quiet her work necessitates and provides.

This year alone she has painted ten watercolors and written a small book of poetry. Now she is working on a map of the retirement community's grounds and buildings.

One evening earlier this spring when Jane, Bob, and I came home, the light on the answering machine was blinking. I pressed the message button, and my mother's voice was in the room, sharing with us her excitement over a new project.

"I need to make my map larger. I've penciled lines an inch apart. What do you think," she asked us, "if I do it by squares? Three-inch squares should enlarge it enough. Or maybe I might just widen the border..."

I ran the message through twice, while the three of us listened. When her voice ended the second time, I turned to put on a light, but first something made me pause. It seemed as if our building, rising on its median between six lanes of traffic, was enfolding us in the dimness and the rare, momentary silence of no cars passing.

20

The dark—unlike death—I have looked at with wide-opened eyes since I was a small child. Like Jane, my oldest sister and I are frightened of it. My two brothers and other sister are not. I suspect they once were until the force of lights off and doors closed at bedtime pushed it underground to other areas. "But, can't fear be an inspiring, motivating force?" I ask myself, not only in my parents' defense but my own because I am beginning to wonder how extensive a role it plays in my life, building impasses and loneliness rather than inspiration.

Although I have shown respect towards Jane's fear by sitting in the darkness of her room for years until she fell asleep, I have denied my own, shutting the door and leaving myself alone in the dark with it. *Hers* seems to have abated. Now, after I say good-night she sometimes goes to sleep with lights out, door closed, and no entreaties for me to stay. There was a time when being frightened made me reach out.

It happened one night on Flamingo when I was eight and alone in the house with Eddie, my younger brother. My mother was up north with the older children, and Eddie and I were under our father's care, although usually at such times we were placed with an aunt. That night, I was awakened by a knocking on the frame of the screen door of our house, the heavier door being left open in the tropical heat. A loud, unnatural voice called out. I woke Eddie, and barefoot we ran down the stairs, out the back door, and over the long, stony road to my aunt's and uncle's house where my father was having supper. He scolded us and immediately drove us home in his truck, saying the night watchman would have sent the inebriated visitor away in another moment or two, which the night watchman had in fact done.

My father did not want his children to be fools or sissies. He did not want them to run away when a night watchman was there to take care of the problem, or to sleep with lights on and doors open, accommodating cowardice. Years later, when he was diagnosed with angina, he knew he might die at any time. But as usual, fear was to be withstood. He closed the door and faced the dark by himself.

At that time on the verge of bankruptcy, he considered himself a failure, but I never discounted his work, generally unrecognized as it was until recently. What he considered his failure, I considered his success and doubted I would do as well. What concerns me more today and keeps me to Bob's and my way of raising Jane is something else. My father was fifty-eight when he died, approximately ten years older than I am now. One evening a couple of months before I graduated from college, I drove home for supper with him and my mother. Afterwards, he walked me to the entrance and stood on the inside of the screen door saying good-night. He gave a humorous, self-deprecatory shrug, but his face, darkened by the screen, was sad and tired. When I came unexpectedly for tea a week later, he had had a heart attack while working in the garden and had died a few hours before. My mother was about to telephone me with the news.

My father's face, looking out that last night from the interior of our fieldstone house, stays with me, and I teach Jane differently than he taught me. I would have praised the scared child holding the hand of her younger brother. And I would say to her this: "Things that cannot be passed by or outgrown (and maybe being scared of the dark will be one of those things for you, as it is for me) can be controlled by a bigger feeling than fear, like feeling responsible for somebody else."

21

If my father spanked me when I was one and a half and drove Eddie and me home in disgrace six and a half years later, when I was five or six, my grandfather left *his* disciplinary mark.

"The first time I went to spend Thanksgiving vacation with my Grandpa and Grandma—Grandma's parents—I was a little younger than you," I volunteer to Jane one afternoon. "On weekends and holidays they lived in the big house above Grandma's. During my visit I felt shy because I didn't know anybody very well yet, neither my cousins, who were also visiting, nor my grandparents. They all knew each other because they spent their summers together while we were on Flamingo.

"Time seemed long to me, but one afternoon a green bullfrog jumped into the small decorative pool on the lawn in back of the house. There, surrounded by light-blue cement walls and toy boats, it proceeded to lay its eggs in the water. I had heard the news and was running towards a porch door when my grandfather caught me by the arm. He said it was time for my nap. When I refused to go to my room, he began to pull me up the long, red, carpeted stairs. My desire to see the frog and my anger that anybody, especially a person I did not know well, would handle me like that, made me fight and kick. My grandfather, used to people obeying him, was equally upset.

"He put me in my room and shut the door. Later, he came back carrying a case of miniature picture-story books.

He lay on my bed and read one after another to me because he regretted losing his temper."

Jane is braiding a French twist into the hair of one of her Barbie dolls.

"Grandpa made a mistake, not so much because he lost his temper, but because there was no good reason why I shouldn't have seen the frog. But I made a bigger mistake because I couldn't forgive him."

I pause to think about that overly tall, thin figure resting awkwardly on my bed reading one tiny book after another to his small grandchild whose face was closed and tear-stained, and I wonder where my heart was, not only then but for the rest of my grandfather's life, for the incident shaded our future together. Simultaneously, it revealed to me my grandfather's temper, nerves, urge to control, and regret — too much for me, a young child, to handle. Recently, when I told Anne about the incident, she said that after our grandfather came back, he should have conceded briefly and sincerely: "I made a mistake. Let's go see if that frog is still there."

I say to Jane, "When I grew older, I realized I had Grandpa's temper. Remembering the bullfrog helps me control it and makes me try harder not to hurt others just because I want my own way. But most of all, it encourages me to be forgiving. Then, I am less frightened of mistakes, mine and other people's, because like magic forgiveness can wipe them out."

"A different way of looking at Grandpa's mistake," I tell myself seven and a half years later when Jane is in tenth grade, "is not as the cause of Grandpa's and my future restraint towards each other but as a shortcut to the truth. Once, rather than never, we appeared vivid and vulnerable before each other."

22

"We weren't brought up to be confident. Neither was our mother," I say to Steven, my older brother, during a visit last summer on Lupin.

"Not many people are," he replies. "Anyway, sometimes confident people are annoying."

Steven likes to argue and is good at it, but I let this call to arms pass. Instead I ask him to confirm a memory I have.

He and I are children, swimming with the others out at Flamingo's airport which consists of a small hangar and short runway. Set off a distance from the hangar, near the road that leads back to town, is a natural pool of water surrounded by large, white stones, the same kind that were crushed to make the runway and roads. The water is opaque green, instead of the normal—for those brackish pools— more transparent brown. Even the brown water, while clear on top, is opaque with any kind of depth. But this water is a thick, chalky green.

Like in a silent film, I swim over to Eddie, four years younger than myself, who is out of his depth, thrashing. His head is tilting back as far as it can go for air, and when I reach him, he climbs blindly on to my shoulders, pushing me under. Although I am Jane's age, I have physically grown and developed faster than she, but I am no match for my brother, wiry as a small monkey and frantic. Above the blurred line of the water and its rocky edge beyond, I see many legs running towards us from the hangar. I am not struggling for air but to keep the line of water from covering my eyes and the vision they cling to. Then I am lying, panting, on the water's edge. I am all right, and nobody is paying attention to me in particular.

"Did that really happen?" I ask Steven.

Yes. Eddie was playing in the shallower water and accidentally stepped into a deep hole. He had just learned how to swim, but panic made him forget. The other children were further away from him than I was. They called for help, and the grownups came running from the hangar.

Sometime after that conversation with Steven I mention the incident to my mother.

She says she was unable to run as fast as she normally did, fear for her son slowing her movements as in a dream, but my father ran his fastest and pulled his two children out.

"We almost lost Eddie," my mother adds and falls silent.

I look at her wonderingly. "You almost lost me too. That water was opaque," I say, "completely opaque. You would not have been able to find us if we had gone under. Eddie was going under when I got to him."

"Yes, you probably saved his life," she concedes.

That we children survived the dangers of island life is a credit to the grownups who watched over us, but it is also a credit to ourselves. There was the ocean we swam in daily, the trees we climbed fast but seldom recklessly, the long bicycle rides to wild, uninhabited spots. We rode in the open backs of trucks, perched on their sides. Bicycle helmets and seat belts were not yet common. In return for our freedom, we were expected in large measure to watch out for ourselves and each other.

So I do not think my mother felt guilty because she or another grownup was not by the swimming hole when Eddie began to drown. Nor that her silence was part of a heritage of withholding praise in order not to make a child vain. I think it was part of a more puzzling, darker heritage.

When my grandmother's brother, as a small boy, proudly exhibited his muscles to his father, his father said, "Those are puny muscles." My grandmother married my grandfather, and shadows of her father's darker side sometimes surfaced in her husband. When my grandfather was old, what he said to his oldest son was often the equivalent of "Those are puny muscles."

My mother, whom my grandfather rarely criticized, fights the shadow of her father's contradictory nature in herself. But these many years later, she still finds both the swimming incident and my part in it difficult to acknowledge. Her praise, however, has been generous about other things I have done, especially after her own work was recognized, and after I married and had a child, two major experiences we have in common. Yet even before then, if at times she neglected to praise, she never said or implied that I fell short.

Until I started writing this book, I did not dwell upon the few images from the past that resided in the back of my mind. Now their significance and power begin to dawn on me. As I start to deal with them, I realize to what a large degree they have colored my idea of a self rarely exposed to the surface. Even as I grasp them more tightly, I suspect they represent a person and past simplified by time. Not that I am so different from the child who resisted her grandfather when he pulled her away from what she wanted to see; or tried to rescue her little brother from drowning; or ran off into the dark with him when she felt a worse danger was near. But the very clarity of those images of taking control, or trying to, speak significantly of forgotten or half-remembered ones of being scared, hesitant, lonely, and shy, qualities that lack of praise might have encouraged and that still shape the surface of my self. Until recently, I discounted their importance, focusing only on my courage.

23

For years I have believed my early childhood was as perfect as Jane's. In telling me what she had seen with her own eyes—my father spanking me when I was one and a half—my sister Susan was implying something else.

"Your insecurities didn't happen overnight, when you turned ten, for instance. They built or were built up slowly," she insisted.

"Sometimes insecurities do happen overnight," I told her. But there was the spanking, which must have helped inhibit my behavior with my father; there was the year I could not read while my classmates could, and the following year when I had to stay behind on Flamingo for tutoring while my older brother went north to school as usual; there was my younger brother's birth, four years after mine, and my mother's attention diverted from me to him. These things happened, but I could not remember them or my reactions. Then I reflected on a memory that seemed insignificant. My tutor once asked me to write a page of "I will pay attention during lessons." Instead, I copied it over for four or five pages. Afterwards, she looked with astonishment and kindness at my overreactive response. Was it a cry for attention that instigated such exaggerated willingness to please? Was it a reaction to my mother being away and separation for the first time from my older brother? As I grew older, did the desire to please expand, growing more and more subtle?

"You used to be such a happy, affectionate child," my mother once wistfully remarked during my rebellion against her in my late twenties. In the few photographs of my early childhood, I am putting my baby arms around her neck, looking at her brightly as she holds me and smiles at the photographer. Or I am playing next to my older brother, the curve of my back touching him. Or I am standing beside Susan, holding her hand. In these photographs I appear confident and affectionate. Even when I cried for the toddler I could not take away with me, I imagine myself walking home, alone with my mother, holding her hand, secure enough to show pain. And, still secure enough to show affection, or maybe it was anxiety, I clearly recall my arms around her that late winter afternoon just before she told me I was too big to hang on her. By then, I was not secure enough to be rejected, even temporarily.

I had suddenly become an awkward, overgrown nine-year-old. I was spending the school year up north in a large house whose rent my parents shared with my two uncles and aunts. For the next four years, until my father left the island and our family moved into its own house, my mother was with him for two-thirds of the school year. Her absence was covered by my aunts: three months each. My older sisters, brother, and cousins eventually went away to boarding schools, but that winter there were eight children, nine during vacations, under the care of either my mother or an aunt. Those school years of living under the same roof caused a bond between us cousins. But teamed up according to age as we were, our brothers and sisters counted for less. Although I was included in their group, I was three years younger than my older brother and a cousin. I played more with Kate, my best friend, but sleepovers were rare and playtime with friends was limited to weekends. Gone was first grade, where the teacher and children celebrated my birthday, and nursery school, when my mother bought and occupied her family's city house That winter, my sisters had measles and were tucked away into darkened rooms on the third floor. Then my father came up from Flamingo and took my mother on a trip around the world. My sisters, well again, went somewhere else. My brother and I roller-skated in the park, while a nurse took care of our younger brother. We were a team for the last time.

From fourth grade on, the timidity and aloofness that marred my social interactions through the first decade of my adulthood rapidly expanded. My teachers, who might have helped, were likewise detached. They were concerned primarily with academics, unlike Jane's elementary or my anonymous first grade instructors. By then, I may have been a child too convoluted and reserved for most teachers to understand. As I did well academically, there seemed no need.

Although my early childhood was a more secure era than my preadolescence, Susan was probably right. Just as my braver acts of the past had cloaked my insecurities, my idyllic moments on Flamingo had made me forget other, less perfect ones there. Loneliness occasionally haunted my time on the island as well as up north, and unpleasant things happened both places. Nature infused Flamingo with a glow that has blinded my perception of this truth.

Both on the island and up north the wider community of my parents, my sisters and brothers and cousins, my aunts and uncles always enfolded me but failed to provide the close attention that might have encouraged more of the affection and social ease I seemed to have possessed as a young child.

Tonight after supper, I would like to watch a video with Bob, or read, or take a bath, but in order to restock my losses as well as to pass on what has been given me, I rise from the sofa to assist Jane with a book project due tomorrow.

24

In her room Jane has decided to make a doll that resembles a character in the book she has read. She starts by cutting out the body and head, arms and legs from a pair of yellow tights I find for her. Under my supervision, she sews the sides of each of these parts together, leaving an opening for the stuffing. To my surprise we discover some cotton in a closet. After filling and sewing the limbs onto the body with my help, Jane wants to draw the face. She practices different versions with magic marker on paper. Then she carefully copies her favorite onto the doll. She hates the result. Abruptly, she stops work. She is not going to make a doll after all but a diorama of a scene in the book, something the children can chose to do instead. Eventually, I cut out another piece from the tights and sew it over the bad face. This time, she uses a ballpoint pen for the features. Then we take turns laboriously sewing on the clothes and hair. At last the doll is finished.

One evening when I am eight or nine, I ride my bicycle out to Flamingo's lighthouse. The light is warm and brilliant, denying the sun's exit in an hour or so. I hear the ocean on the other side of the bushes spreading itself out thinly on strips of beach and then withdrawing, or lapping and echoing under low, gray and black coral cliffs.

When I reach the lighthouse, I climb the metal steps inside, up through nebulous space filled with underwater light. At the top I open the door and step out onto the landing. There is the edge of green running along the road next to the sea, while on the other side, stretching into the distance, are the dusty greens and grays of the flat, wild land. I turn back to stare at another expanse of almost formless space: the sea barely divided from the sky or from the sun still flaring and blue at its center. The movement of a small object on land distracts me; a familiar station wagon is traveling down the road towards the lighthouse. The sight scares me, as I know it carries my mother, and I am not allowed to be where I am.

I do not remember any other blatantly disobedient act in my childhood. My mother does not remember the incident, so it remains a mystery. Whether I am good, medium, or bad, I cannot help being an artist, in the same way that child is drawn to the lighthouse and the freedom and beauty it offers.

But am I alone on that high landing, or is someone with me? As I recall the unwavering approach of my mother's car,

I am suddenly sure my friend Mary, the minister's daughter, is standing next to me.

The doll is displayed at school with the other book projects and then comes home to sit on top of Jane's bookcase. Like the butter churn, its beauty is only visible to a few. Whenever I look at it, I am reminded of our struggles and the moments of satisfaction we found together along the way and at the end.

25

Now the book project assignment is a year ahead of me, and I am looking back six months to that first day of school when Jane thought she could not read and asked me if I could at her age. "I can't remember much about when I was your age, just a few flashes here and there, but I remember when I first learned how. It must have happened all of a sudden because to this day I can recall the joy of that moment."

"When did you learn?"

"I was supposed to be reading in first grade, but I wasn't, and I wrote everything backwards. If you held my writing up to a mirror, it was perfect. According to my mother, I hid my disability from everyone, memorizing what I could. Toward the end of the school year she discovered my secret. I don't remember her immediate reaction, but that summer and the following winter there was an instructor on the island who taught me to read and write correctly."

"Were you unhappy in first grade?"

"No, I was happy, particularly one day when I was given birthday cards and little favors. I carried them home from school and explained to my mother, who stopped to listen at the stairs' landing on her way down to see me, that my teacher and class had celebrated my birthday. My mother was glad for me, although she had forgotten the event herself.

"I don't remember being in the least upset by her forgetfulness. I was happy and excited with all the attention from school and wanted to share my happiness with her.

"Another day, earlier that year, I returned from school and, to my surprise and disappointment, there was no mother to greet me. Then I saw a small table pushed to the center of the hall with a lamp shining on a note and one fancy chocolate. The chocolate sat in its ribbed, darker brown wrapper. I don't know what the note said. Remember, I couldn't read, and my mother didn't discover that until some months later. But the image of the chocolate and the note under the light has stayed with me to this day."

Throughout my life when I have been in trouble, my mother has sensed it, even if I have tried to hide it from her. Even from a distance she has sensed it, from a line in a letter, or a tone of voice on the phone. Everything of lesser importance between us is dropped, and she sends me something or says or does something, each the equivalent or more of placing a chocolate and note under a lamp. So she brightens the darkness that has temporarily besieged me.

26

While my mother was devoted to her children, my father came first. When I was a baby and again when I was a small child, old enough to remember waking at night from a nightmare, she left me in order to travel extensively with him. She left all of us children for periods of time to be with her husband, as her mother had done. Her father had had a thick wall built between the parents' and babies' quarters, so her mother would not hear her babies cry at night. Those cries were for nannies to subdue.

In love with my father as she was, my mother wanted to be with him, but after Jane was born, she offered another reason why she had left me when her husband needed her: the example of a happy marriage was one of the most valuable gifts parents could give their children. Whether that was her reasoning at the time or not, her behavior may have been for the best, considering the geographical and psychological demands of her life with my father.

I believe my parents' marriage was a happy one, but, growing up, I did not take much note of that distant phenomenon. Its romantic and strife-free nature obscured its reality for me and made the complexities of my parents' separate personalities hazier. I never saw the two fight, and my mother assures me that once married they never did. Looking back, she describes herself and my father as "two innocents." But, like my sister Anne, my mother is not an innocent. Unlike my father, who tried to be a realist and not be swept away by ideas that lacked substance, she has always reached for romance.

It was my father who gravely remarked to me that marriage was full of small sacrifices: if each of the two participants gave seventy percent, it might work. Both he, romantic as he was, and my mother, appreciative of romance as she was, practiced the nitty-grittiness those words preached, and the attention and sacrifices their marriage inspired between them were real enough and blurred the line between what they gave each other and what they gave their children.

When Jane was keen on Walt Disney's *The Little Mermaid* and wanted to rent the movie for the fourth time, I said to her, "I like some of the songs, but I just want to be sure you understand one of the main messages that is being given out here."

"What messages?" asked my first grader blankly.

"Well, the little mermaid is the one doing all the sacrificing. What about the prince?"

"That's the little mermaid's decision," replied Jane without missing a beat.

Disney's little mermaid and her prince both had kings and queens as parents, as my mother and father did, so to speak. But my parents' two kingdoms were similar; my mother did not have to shed a fish tail for my father and grow legs and feet. Living on the island, however, was profoundly different from either of their pasts. It was my father's choice to settle there, but my mother chose my father as her ideal and embraced his new world as one that fulfilled her own fantasies. I can understand Jane's viewpoint better now because I never had the sense that my mother's life with my father was controlled in ways that she minded.

"Before we got married, we fought all the time," my mother said, "because your father was a Republican from a Republican family, while my family and I were Democrats and voted for Roosevelt." The significance of what she has told us children a number of times since we were little did not sink in until recently: my mother was liberal, my father conservative. Since my mother in certain key aspects refused to cross my father, their marriage was on the more traditional side, and that is how we were raised. Boys made money; girls married and did art and music and writing on the side. We all graduated from elite schools and colleges. Marketing my labor never crossed my mind in a real sense, even when I was forced for a couple of years to work in an office. I wanted to perfect the art I did, but to get it out into the world in conspicuous ways would invite a loveless life.

When my father and his two brothers decided they had failed not only to make money on their business venture but were headed towards losing the rest of the family fortune, they sold the salt-making operation to a bigger company. My mother with her liberal views fought against my father's despair and sense of failure, claiming that he with his brothers' help had orchestrated a successful effort to put an economy back on its feet by providing training, jobs, long-range plans, and inspiration. If my father could have looked into the future, he would have seen Flamingo today as a supporting but critical branch—run entirely by the local population—of a major salt-making company and the only prosperous island among its neighbors. What he saw instead was family money lost rather than doubled or tripled.

In my late twenties I returned briefly to the island with my uncle and aunt, their daughter, and her family. At that time in my life I thought less about my childhood there than about my mother and father and their life together. The loading and shipping had been removed to outside the town's boundaries, and without the passing trucks and the centering salt pile in front of our house, a sense of the overwhelming isolation grabbed me.

If Jane, as an adult, stands in my present studio, where already I have worked for over ten years, a similar pang might strike her. After hours Bob and I go out and see people, if only to do errands, but Jane may sense, especially if I and my paintings are absent, that although her mother does not work on a small island, on another level she does, even as her grandparents did.

After selling the business, my father and his two brothers went their separate ways, and my father, leader that he had been, was not only without followers but also without the support and restraining presence of his older brother and of the islanders themselves. Apart from his imaginative side, my father was conservative not only in his private life but in his approach to work, overworking most of his adult life and rarely taking vacations. But his hands had a liberalism that escaped his head, and when physical labor with others was no longer an integral part of the overall picture, he moved out of his depth. I remember him best working outdoors beside the men he was paying. The dry heat invigorated him as the cold up north never did, and he would strip to shorts, hat, dark glasses, socks, and sneakers whenever he could.

Certain events of my father's life distracted my mother from his conservatism and ultimately removed her opposition to him, resulting in their engagement. A brief rebellion occurred on the island. My father was shot with a sawed-off shotgun and passed four severely uncomfortable days on the ocean with no food and little water. Because of guns in the boat, he and the fourteen other men of his party ended up in a Cuban prison. The proper authorities were eventually reached, and all released. This close call melted my mother's heart.

Before marrying my father, my mother had adventures too. In the tropics she wore dresses with long sleeves and hats against the sun, but, as a child and young woman, cold weather and high altitude were what energized her. Horses, animals my father did not care for and nonexistent on Flamingo, were her love. Although not athletic in the general sense, she grew up riding with a friend over her father's and his family's merging estates in the country.

She was also surprisingly good at skiing. One of the earlier downhill skiers in the country, she once refused a request to try out for the Olympic team. In her early twenties, while traveling in Europe, she and a friend went on a skiing trip. The altitude made her friend sleep longer but jolted my mother awake earlier than usual like an electric shock and dulled her sense of caution. Each morning she would find herself setting out in the dawn's fog. One day she skied to a hut high up where three countries met. Another time she fell and when she stopped, her head was over a crevice.

My father's love of parties during his college years resulted in his at least once attending his morning classes with a coat thrown over the prior evening's dress clothes. For twenty-five years he turned his back on a style of living he enjoyed in order to realize a dream. When it failed, he moved back up north and commuted by train to a city office. On summer weekends he often worked in the garden. During those last ten years he joined but never used several exclusive city clubs. His sense of failure may have doused any real movement in that direction. My mother, perhaps discouraged by him and by the nature of the wealthy suburban town in which we lived, also made little social effort. But after his death she joined a garden club and contributed by making signs in calligraphy on found pieces of wood and illustrating them with painted birds.

Here we are, she said to my father in so many words, we have each other and with luck years ahead in which to travel and see our children and grandchildren. Outside of business, you have many accomplishments and interests: the mural we painted for our daughters' and niece's graduation dance; the large saltwater tank you stocked with exotic tropical fish and took care of as a teenager; aviation when you were in your twenties and thirties, including the skill to fly yourself under a bridge. What about all those years of playing the piano? It interested you before, why not now? Few people know as much about growing roses as you do. What if we have to move to a smaller house? There is enough on hand for retirement. Don't put what you have left into a risky venture.

But that is what he did. After his death my mother hired a lawyer who eventually retrieved some of the profits, being kept hidden from our family, on the ship he had helped finance.

My mother left college after a year in order to start searching for the right man to marry. Over the next few years she gave and attended parties and compared suitors carefully in her mind. Since I first heard this information about her past, I have not doubted her grasp of reality along certain lines, hidden as it is to many people's eyes. She picked as her romantic ideal a man who was on an equal economic footing with her, who appreciated her artistic ability, and supported her desire to have a family. He was her primary consultant while she raised the five children she had dreamed of having. And the island gave birth to some of her best watercolors and calligraphy.

Less clear about what I wanted, the one thing I was sure I did not want was to be dominated, and I put off marriage for many years in large part because of that fear.

"Why are you marrying him?" my friend's husband had asked me.

"Because I can get angry at him," I had replied in jest but with the secret conviction that therein lay the source of my freedom.

Bob is similar to my father in many respects. Essentially a romantic as the latter was, he did not marry a woman like my mother, who, while maintaining a firm grip on reality, looks for romance. Instead he married me, another romantic like himself at times tempted by vaporous leanings. As a result, Bob and I are conscious to the quick of not turning each other into romantic ideals. A sense of personal freedom was one of Bob's first attractions for me, although I could not articulate it other than to say "I can get angry at him." On the surface our marriage is more mundane than my parents' was. We fight and often put Jane before ourselves, in part because she is important proof of our union.

Once or twice a year, before Jane was born, we spent the day in bed together, resting and talking. My mother smiled when she inadvertently discovered our laziness.

"Your father and I used to do that when we couldn't get away," she said.

When my mother first talked to me as an equal, I was in my late twenties. She and I were walking on her childhood mountain with tall trees standing on a curve of ground above us. I forget what she said, but behind her words was an opening that led to a relationship of my own with her and eventually helped to free me for Bob.

Her remark offers another reason why she chose my father. "I liked your father to chase me," she once disclosed to me. An image of an unclothed male with sunburned body, which during the Flamingo years my father's inevitably was, chasing a white nymph flashes across my mind. But as beautiful and elegant as past photographs claim my mother to have been, they hide a certain frankness of hers about the body. It manifests itself in how she talks about her children's births; how she squeezes her grapefruit impetuously, without fastidiousness; how she sang comparatively loudly in church the few times we went, relishing life and the hymns and the sound of her voice and embarrassing me, a child, because of her difference from the others.

One photograph of my mother, taken by her nanny, *is* different. A young girl sits on a swing with a bow in her hair, a corsage on her sweater, her hands relatively big, awkward, and real on the ropes of the swing. There is a vulnerability about the child, paused for a second in her swinging and being photographed by somebody who loved her and whom she loved, which gives me a pang. I wonder less about how often my mother might have showed this side of herself and more about how rarely I have seemed able to expose a similar one in my work or otherwise. Ironically, the only time my looks have been declared similar to my mother's was when a friend insisted this photograph resembled a painting of me at about the same age.

My mother left my father for three months during the school year to be with her children, and he left her during the war and later while traveling on business. Often Bob leaves me or I him when we are concentrating on Jane or on our work. If the isolation of physical absence dominated my mother's marriage, that of periodic mental distance dominates my own. It separates Bob and me but also draws us together. Lying as it does at each of our centers, we recognize and accept it in the other to a generous extent. We fight it only when, now and then, it becomes too extreme.

My mother's desire to romanticize my father may have resulted in fewer arguments but also encouraged some of my father's limitations. In regard to certain issues such as the isolation of their last ten years together, could my mother have crossed my father more? Although she had advised him against his last business venture, he had not listened. Neither of them were accustomed to her taking a stand in such matters.

My father's mother, arguably even closer to my father than my mother, supplied a major part of the financial support for the salt-making project to the extent that she had to worry about maintaining her lifestyle in her old age. A second mother to my mother and idealized by both her son and daughter-in-law, she at least once told my father what to do. Change your tie, she told him one night before dinner when, as usual on our way to and from Flamingo, we were staying over with her in Nassau. And he did. Only she may have had that power over him. But my mother's influence was strong and in some important ways untapped.

When I questioned my uncle, he told me bad weather and the construction of a magnesium plant caused the salt-making effort to fail. Magnesite, a substance used in making steel, was to help with the war effort. But the demand had fallen, and more exhaustive research had uncovered problems. In *Great Inagua*, a book about those times, my mother wrote that Flamingo's limestone crumbled too easily for the kilns built, and the manufacturing process required more of the island's scarce supply of fresh water than anticipated. The plant's failure to go into production was "no one's fault but came about because the undertaking was so complicated and new it could not be investigated thoroughly ahead of time" (page 168). But my uncle blamed himself, claiming the idea had been his to adequately research and supervise.

We children were prohibited from exploring those new, unused concrete buildings with their alluring cool spaces and interesting mechanical objects. But we were free to play in the other cause of the brothers' eventual business defeat: the rain. We would run outside to rapturously greet those rare, hard downpours. Wearing only our bathing suits and sneakers, we joined the land crabs who were escaping dark, flooded holes. Our houses were humid and dark too, our mothers having closed the shutters over the screens, and the airless, dim interiors were as strange to them in the daytime as the gray sky.

When it rained, my father may have worked on one of

his inventions like how to shoot salt higher over the salt piles; or written business and family letters for the next mail boat; or he may have driven around the pans, either changing gates according to the conditions—unless they made such activity futile—or looking for low land to expand the salt-making area. He sometimes appeared at home to take a hot shower before leaving again, his eyes naked without his dark glasses.

In order to back the ship, whose profits my mother's lawyer eventually salvaged, my father needed cash, so he sold his shares in the salt company he had pioneered. One stick breaks, he used to say about himself and his brothers, more easily than three bunched together. Yet it was his family that broke as well as made him. The brothers' three-way marriage ended when the company made good. My uncle explained to me that he had warned my father against pulling out, but his advice was ignored. He claimed that when my father gave up his shares, he put the company at risk. When the latter was unexpectedly sold a short time later, neither he nor my younger uncle nor the third partner, my father's best friend, felt obligated to further split the gains, which far exceeded the amount my mother cleared, several years after my father died, from the ship venture.

I used to wonder if my father in his brothers' shoes would have acted accordingly. But he was a babe in the woods, as my grandfather put it. Besides, where would it have ended if the other three had been generous? Would my mother have shared with them the ship's profits? What about the magnesium plant? Was its failure in truth my uncle's fault, and the capital subsequently lost owed the other two? Because my father was the instigator of the salt-making effort, should he have reimbursed his mother and brothers for the dissolved, major portion of the family fortune? Did his vision save or waste his siblings' talents? Depending on the answer, what was his debt to them in this regard or theirs to him?

Do I owe my father unfinished paintings? Do I hit a glass ceiling when I approach the end of a painting because I cannot pass him or my mother, my sisters or brothers, my husband, or even my daughter and risk leaving them behind?

Yet a marriage involving the substance of my work's main focus over the past fifteen years with any of the people who mean most to me would be incompatible. Despite their strong overall support, they are not the viewers who most appreciate the still lifes. The energy it takes to override my inclination to please them may play a subtle part in my struggle to finish work. And occasionally, not so subtle. Once, in the face of Bob's dislike of a canvas, I painted over it.

Stretching and preparing more canvases; working on more than one at a time; sending out slides and exhibiting more often; setting up more deadlines. These are good ideas, but I have not been able to carry them out.

So, it is in the murkier area of psychology where I have bogged down and why at this minute I am writing instead of painting. Over-romanticizing may lead to blindness, and blindness to not taking a stand, and not taking a stand to tragedy, but the isolation I write off as being recognized and accepted by Bob and me may be an excuse—as much as my parents' tendency to romanticize may have been—for invulnerability. And that resulting, certain lack of inner attention towards each other and our own selves may end in not taking a stand when necessary. Not so much concerning the big things as the smaller. As a couple, what people do Bob and I see, what movies or television programs, what interior decorations do we decide on, who decides? In areas where one is more skilled or motivated, the other must still take notice and at times be heard and accommodated because it all affects who I, for instance, am and the work I do.

27

During the summer following fourth grade I read *Little Women* for the first time. My fantasies about love and sex were grounded in Jo's relationship with Larry, whom she spurned in the end; Larry's successful courtship of Amy, the youngest sister; and Jo's denouement with her stout, bearded professor. The moment she turned to kiss him under an umbrella in the rain was "the crowning moment of both their lives." My own putting of sex on a pedestal was compounded by my mother's but particularly my father's view that sex before would result in faithlessness after marriage.

During my senior year in college I was taken with D.H. Lawrence and chose to write a term paper on *Women in Love*. Sex was a mysterious, ultimately impersonal force of nature.

The few men who won my confidence resisted being turned into forces of nature and fought my inclination to over-romanticize sex. But still I was inclined towards a mixed attitude: with myself I was relaxed; with another less so since I considered sex inseparable from love and eventually marriage. But the latter situation also restrained me for a more negative reason: my belief that the less vulnerable one was, the better the sex.

For many of my single years I romanticized beyond any physical returns, having fallen in love with a man who could not bring himself to tell me he was gay, either because he thought he might be bisexual or because whenever he began to explain, I was too unsuspecting to help him along. Not ready to settle down, I may have been willfully blind.

During those years there was no sex with another person, an experience which taught me not only the value of finding somebody compatible in that respect, but the ultimate fallowness for me of too much romanticizing regarding a mate.

With Jane being a young child and our trying to fit in her demands with those of our work, combined with the relative lack of privacy at home, sex is still enjoyed but my own focus of attention often neglects it. I take a more passive role: when asked, I generally acquiesce and then am glad I did.

My initial reluctance may have less to do with limited opportunities than with a misconception I have in common with finishing paintings. Sex does not have to include everything each time, any more than does a painting. There are

other paintings, other times to make love: this is the way it is this time.

Suddenly, here is this chapter being concluded without effort on a subject I would have thought even a short time ago too personal to write about or paint.

28

The leaves are now full size, darker, and multitudinous. They tend to overlap each other, flat and pointy with inner or outer curves. Their mass, movement, and sound are a soothing change from earlier in the spring. Then, I had just begun to write, not these pages yet but the ones for my talk about being an artist. As I struggled with first one word then another, I was aware of the leaves outside, each a tiny point, then a separate miniature of its grown self, silently and rapidly unfurling and growing.

At this time, a few months later, my words start to come more easily. Now and then, I am hardly aware of them, wrapped up as I am in what I want to say, and you, dear reader, are less the enemy and more the receptive air around them.

Lying under my desk by my feet, our dog Homer shifts his position. I bend down to pat him and then sit motionless, a feeling of grief, like a strange paralysis, spreading through me. After an instant or two, the intensity fades. I look around for my pencil, seeking the comfort of reaching inside myself to find and gently pull out a spool of tape in order to see what is written there.

29

Early this spring I noticed a swelling on the outside of Homer's gum next to his back teeth. The vet examined it and called to say it was cancer. Bob and I explained to Jane that Homer would most likely die this summer or next fall, although he seemed well. In the beginning we fussed over him, but soon our household returned to its normal routine. My lack of concern when I first spotted the irregularity, hardly noticeable and soon removed, stayed with me.

Ten years ago, we were recently married and in another city for the weekend when, upon our exiting a museum, there was Homer, eager to take us on. We had not discussed having a dog, but after we made inquiries, we drove off with our new family member.

Once back at our place, Homer explored our kitchen, dining room, living room, hall, bathroom, bedroom, and smaller bedroom. He moved with assurance and excitement over his new human home. Bad behavior was limited to his suddenly rising onto his hind legs and snatching the thick, inedible skin of a fish off the kitchen counter before swallowing it whole.

Almost two years later I became pregnant with Jane. During our three weeks on Lupin Bob left Homer and me to attend a wedding back home. For those two clear, calm evenings I sat on the porch with a cold, and the ledges of the rocks, uncovered at low tide, pulled the flatness of the sea up close so that I could comprehend its distance better. It was early summer, but I felt an August premonition of fall. I glanced at Homer nearby and thought how lonely the landscape would have been without his presence.

Even after Jane arrived, late the following winter, and my attention swung away from Homer to her, I continued to feel a particular kinship with our stray who, when he first greeted us, had leapt gracefully into the air over and over again as if trying both to reach our human level and to express a wild animal's sense of well-being.

Although I walked him every evening, I no longer took him around the reservoir. I rarely played with him, nor did I drive him to my studio on my car days but instead left him home for Bob to take out after lunch. Despite Bob's extra attention, Homer missed mine, and during Jane's early years he lay under her crib, pressed back against the wall, his posture and movements those of a rejected animal.

From his first days with us he exhibited certain fears, but these seemed to expand rapidly after Jane. She was not yet walking when I noticed that if a curtain moved in front of an open window, Homer would freeze in his tracks and start to shake or, at the sight of a blown-up balloon, cringe and withdraw. Faced with a mistress who suddenly seemed unable to find time for him but who did not hesitate to rise three or four times during the night to take another non-talking creature into her arms, Homer began to succumb to night fears too. After quieting Jane and drifting off to sleep, I might be disturbed again by four feet planted around my face and fast, nervous pants breathing down on me. Some years later, a pet, caged guinea pig, spending the weekend with us, was hastily sent over to a friend's because its presence brought on terror and bouts of diarrhea. But the inconvenience and discomfort that such fears have caused us over the years are minor compared to what Homer's two biggest ones, related more directly to people, have cost.

During his first visit to the vet's, Homer omitted any

warning sign before slashing at the vet's hand when it reached under his body to examine him. Although he was not bitten, the vet advised getting rid of the dog, which we seriously considered but did not do. Thereafter, however, we watched him closely; taught Jane, when she came along, to be careful; and shrank from the approaching dates of his checkups and shots. As he seemed less threatened by females, I was the one to take him into the examining room and muzzle him, whereupon he would erupt into a hostile frenzy. An assistant and I had to hold him as the vet worked, and my shirt was wet by the visit's end.

This year a new vet took a look at the situation. "I think this dog wants to please you. You are saying 'good dog' to reassure him, but instead you are encouraging him to defend himself. Tell him 'no' when he growls."

Homer still verges on hyperventilating in the waiting room, and in the examining room cries pitifully, but, confronted with my stern voice, his desire to please me fights his apprehension and keeps him from turning into the violent creature that nobody wants to handle.

Most haunting of all his fears is that of being abandoned. Nervous when crowded or petted too much, he nonetheless follows me tirelessly around, settling down completely in each room I occupy, however temporarily. When I am away, he follows Bob. Even in Maine with all its space he stays close to us except when Alice, Bob's sister, or other dogs come to visit. If we leave the island without him and he manages to escape from the house, he runs along the seaweed-covered rocks by the water's edge at a dangerous, frantic pace, attempting to follow the departing boat, all the while giving loud, almost human voice to his panic—an unseemly sound for a dog to make.

In all probability abandoned at seven months—the vet's approximation of his age when we first brought him in—

over two and a half years later he was partially abandoned by me, his primary caregiver, and taken over by Bob, whose experience and increased commitment accomplished a good deal but counted for less than my desertion.

The only hiatus from Homer's loneliness occurred when our family went away, and he stayed with Alice. When we returned, he would slowly climb our building's stairs as if he regretted leaving the place where he had received the female attention he craved.

In those days, as my activities on Lupin were curtailed by a baby Jane, he would sometimes leave my side and follow Alice around when she came. One time, in his possessiveness of her, he attacked her dog. I pulled him away and hit him. Bristling and snarling, he escaped from me and disappeared. His sudden belligerent behavior caught Alice by surprise too, and she tentatively suggested that he was getting spoiled. "That's not the trouble," I said. "That's not the trouble at all. He gets way too little attention, way too little."

I found him upstairs under Bob's and my bed. When I entered the room, I heard a growl. Heedlessly, I dropped to my hands and knees to look under the bed. A few inches from my face Homer stared out at me, growling, an animal turned wild with hurt. The desire to punish left me, and I lay down on my side, curved toward him, and talked to him. Soon Jane would grow older and sleep through the night, I told him. Then I would have more time for him. Soothed by my voice, he quieted and inched closer. Finally, he crawled out and shook himself.

Jane's early years passed, and, as she grew, she courted Homer. As I became less tired, I gave him more attention. Now in the morning he helps me wake Jane. He nudges her and wags his tail, behavior which is a compliment, as he tends to wag his tail only when nervous.

But the years of my emotional abandonment along with my inability still to give him as much attention as I first did have taken their toll. Long ago he stopped lying close to me when I am sick. Although I am as always his beloved mistress, his love, for the most part, has grown aloof and reserved, reminding me of myself.

Didn't I too for some years feel emotionally deserted by my mother? And was it Jane's arrival alone that detached me from my dog child, or was it in part the young growing older? In a few years will I feel like shaking off Jane's arms around me, as my mother did mine, as I shook off Homer?

After we learned Homer was going to die soon, I could not forgive myself for the years I had neglected him. Even Alice stood accused of not understanding the nature and extent of his feeling for her. Looking back over his life, all I could see was a lonely dog under a baby's crib. Then it crossed my mind that imperfection was not only part of life but something to be expected, and my bitterness passed.

Now I remember the times Homer has been happy: outside mostly. Walking soothes his being, as it does my own, and he blends into nature like a fox or coyote, two animals he somewhat resembles. If he is attacked by another dog, he fights back, warily sometimes, but he never shakes or runs away. Even a guinea pig, outdoors, does not faze him.

One weekend, three bitches visited Lupin, and for a moment during that happy time the two sides of Homer's nature seemed to meet: his sensitivity to nature and to people. The dogs ran all over the island together, appearing now and then for food and drink. During one of the afternoons, Homer materialized before me out of the thick, warm fog that had settled in the area. His wet fur, his body, his eyes, all expressed joy. He gave me a look and slow wave of his tail, and then the visit was over. He was gone to find the others waiting for him on the rocks or in the woods.

How will it be when he is really gone? I remember Alice's grief during the week after her dog died. I envied how she could cry so hard in the face of death. But I have cried over other endings and departures, or imagined ones. When I thought Bob had decided to call off our relationship, I cried through an afternoon. Buying food for supper, I cried as I handed money to the cashier. Another time, just after Bob and I started sharing living quarters, my mother came for a brief visit. Still residing on her mountainside in another state, she came and left by train. At the visit's end we drove her to the station, helped her onto the train with her luggage, and watched it disappear down the tracks. When we returned to our car, a sense of my mother's loneliness and of my separation from her overwhelmed me.

If I have not cried over certain people who have died, perhaps it is because I do not think of them as dead. My grandparents and father, at the time of his death, were not part of my daily existence, and when they died, their absence may have seemed only longer than usual. If I had seen them no longer alive, that illusion might have ceased to exist. Then again, it might not have. Yet, although I have not mourned them, the dead at times strike like lightning out of the cloud of my forgetfulness and exert influence.

When Alice cried for her dog, she may have been crying not only for him but for the years of her life his spanned. His death may have marked the end of her children's infancy and childhood with such finality that no illusion could remain. At the end of my dog child's life I may look back and see what he has taught me about control: how "bad dog" was correct to say when he misbehaved at the vet's but wrong after I hit him.

Then too, I see myself kneeling before a snarling, frightened animal to put on a muzzle or doing other such acts that signify courage and caring and help define me as much as him.

Most of all, through Homer I have learned that a mistake —like emotionally forsaking an animal for a few years— does not cancel out what I have given or what has been given to me. With the absorption of this truth, my casual reaction to Homer's illness begins to fade.

I tend to toss my fears off as trivial, surface things, but my writing hand knows better, and from the beginning these pages have returned repeatedly to those trepidations, not insignificant but powerful, that were beginning to rule me in my work and life and hold me back. They stem, as Homer's seem to, in large part from a heightened sensitivity to what are often temporary human feelings.

30

During my single years I devoted myself to a few close friends. Keeping friends was always easier than making new ones, especially after leaving school. Bob had a wide circle of acquaintances when I met him, and as a couple we made several new friends under his guidance. But last fall it crossed my mind that even before Bob, I had rarely, if ever, been the initiator.

When I first knocked on Amy's studio door shortly after meeting her over a year ago, she appeared before me, curt and impatient. As a rule, I dislike being disturbed at work, and, not knowing me well, she probably assumed I was going to be intrusive. Stella, Ravenna's mother, neglected to answer a casual invitation.

In the face of Amy's and Stella's apparent disinterest, I withdrew into my own doubts. My principal one concerned the small amount of time I felt able to spend with friends, old or new. But, although I had not yet deliberated upon the matter, the number of Jane's friends had inspired the beginning of a new attitude on my part. It also had given birth to a decision, as unconscious and tentative as it was, to try and avoid the degree of commitment I had until then associated with friendship, even in its early stages. If I chose wrong, I would move on. After confronting my own ambivalence, my sensitivity to one friend's curtness and the other's silence abated. Later, when Amy asked me to her studio and Stella to her house, I accepted their invitations without resentment.

I see neither Amy nor Stella on a daily or even weekly basis and rarely in the telling confines of both home and work-place. But occasionally Amy and I exchange studio visits, or we spend an afternoon having lunch, then seeing galleries. Our time together is infrequent yet offers mutual comprehen-sion and support. So far, it is an easy, rewarding friendship.

Stella and I are more competitive. The resolve to avoid difficult friendships at this time—as rewarding as they can be—has been thwarted by my growing involvement with Ravenna. Something had claimed Stella's attention, making her unhappy, and her unhappiness was claiming Ravenna's. I tried to help the daughter in muted, psychological ways, and the mother responded by inviting me, or Bob and me, or Jane, Bob, and me, or Jane to special social events at her house. But from the beginning issues of control have domi-nated our relationship.

Last winter, Stella gave a talk on an historic heroine of hers. By then, I knew she was debating whether to get divorced. Her heroine, whom I will call Virginia, also struggled with a difficult marriage but had stayed with her husband. After the talk I found I could not congratulate the lecturer despite a job well done. Although I had my own literary heroine, Jo March, I had refused, albeit belatedly, to let her dictate over my life. The suggestion I heard under-lying Stella's speech was that her own life had run, was running, and should run a course parallel to Virginia's. I decided the admiration she had for her heroine was blinding her to her situation and to who she was at a decisive period in her life. We had spent little time alone together and rarely talked intimately, but I knew she was making a mis-take I had almost made. During the refreshment period I took it upon myself to point out the discrepancy between her concept of Virginia and a hymn Virginia had written. It was one Stella loved and had asked the audience to sing.

"This hymn," I declared, "is in praise of war, but you are publicly and outstandingly against war and claim Virginia was too." Surprise may have silenced any reasonable reply.

Stella's glowing face as she talked about Virginia had upset me on another level: if she could not see Virginia's reality, how could she see mine? Yet I have often failed in the past to see my friends' and vice-versa. Only recently have Kate and I begun to comprehend each other's shortcomings.

Some time after the talk I mentioned Stella's name to a friend, thinking she might like to meet her. But she already had once and remembered her unfavorably. "She isn't what you would call a warm person," she remarked.

"I think she is," I said slowly and then paused, struck by a sudden truth. "Well, if she isn't, neither am I." If Stella and I sometimes seem to lack a certain warmth, what inspires our lack? Being too controlling or controlled? Having too great a desire for perfection?

Jane's and Ravenna's friendship remains strong. Stella and I still see each other but more warily than before, and our rare moments of intimacy tend to show themselves in a negative light. As my criticism must have hurt Stella after her talk, in various, small ways she seems unaware of, she has hurt me. Recently, she asked me to take a child, a visitor from another country, on one of my daily walks with Homer. I refused. "Walking Homer is part of the workday," I explained. "I try to think about work then." At the moment I was disinclined to help. Another time I would have enjoyed doing so. But how could I have said no to a friend asking such a small favor?

Especially to Stella, who always tried to grant my requests immediately. But hers, somewhat more frequent than mine, were sometimes difficult for me to disconnect from a sense of being manipulated. Did she think that by making me serve her she was more in control? Or did she believe that the measure of friendship lay in the extent to which friends served each other?

When I objected to her request, her expression hardened, and she turned away. "You must work very hard."

"I do," I said. Didn't Stella, who worked hard herself, grasp that about me?

A short time later, when Bob was away, I invited her with her children to supper. She called at the last minute to ask, did I mind if she did not come but sent the children? Sensing my surprise, she came but then left, as soon as the meal was over, to attend a meeting at a mutual friend's house. As she had picked the date of the supper, I was confused. I had asked her over thinking a more intimate relationship between us was still possible. Perhaps that was *her* way of saying no.

"Don't attempt to read other people's minds," Bob sometimes says to me.

"Try to," I respond.

Jane, caught in the middle, will adopt one philosophy or the other, depending on which is to her advantage at the moment. "Don't try to read my mind," she will answer me when I say she is tired, and it is time for bed. But if she accuses her father of something and he says, "Don't try to read my mind," she will say, "Mommy says it is good to try."

When Jane says to me, "Don't try to read my mind," she is in part saying, "Don't try to control me." And when she accuses her father of something, she is in part trying to control him. Stella's erratic behavior regarding me may be similarly motivated. "I'm sorry you're surprised," she seems to be saying to me, "but if you can't understand me, then you can't control me."

"If I can't understand you, then I can't be sympathetic. Be clear and direct," I want to counter. The threat of being pulled back into a world I am trying to escape makes me as sharp with Stella at times as she is with me, but on the other hand I am often aware of how she is feeling, even if I cannot read her mind.

Last summer she came to Lupin to pick up Ravenna. During her short visit she sat on the porch and sketched the view. When she took the girls drawing, I saw the three huddled together on some distant rocks. The girls' positions seemed protective of her in a way I could not seem to be, and their drawings, when they brought them back, seemed inspired.

Although a friendship of the minds that I have found so easily with Amy eludes Stella and me so far, there is this bond between us. Over the past year in our attempts to realize it, we have hurt more than helped each other, for reasons I have tried to understand.

I write "tried to understand" in deference to Bob's point of view. I do not know Stella well. I am not qualified to read her mind. Am I qualified to read anybody's, even my best friend Kate's, or Bob's, Jane's, or my mother's? Perhaps not, but sensitivity to how people are feeling is something special to possess that could lead towards becoming a warmer person rather than to withdrawal, as for me it often has. Attempting to read minds may ultimately be a superfluous part of the process but as yet seems to offer guidance to the sensitivity. Valid enough, I tell Bob, as long as I realize how mistaken my conclusions may be.

Having initially chosen Amy and Stella, whether our friendships grow or not, I have begun to expand my world of choice. Next time the process should be easier and more on the mark, if need be. Who chooses whom first can be semantics, of course, but reaching out—as I reached out to Amy and Stella—is not.

The real waste for me is to put others on pedestals or let myself be so placed, and Stella's and my spears may ultimately be attempts to crack the other's stand in order to see if we have anything in common on the level.

A yet greater waste is that child, out of an exaggerated desire to please, laboriously writing out her punishment for pages beyond what is due.

31

Because of my own social struggles and because of the emphasis Jane's schools placed on socialization, I have assumed Jane to be more and myself less advanced socially than we are. I may have fewer friends not only because, like Jane, I am shy, but because I am less interested in many.

There is much we can learn together. My admiration for her friends has already influenced me. As for her, at least once a year she takes a train with me to visit Kate. During those weekends does she notice the degree of commitment that still exists between us?

Sometimes an adult asks Jane, "Who's your best friend?" Jane, unwilling or unable to explain about her best friends, will answer, "Cary," or "Jessica," or "Ravenna," or "Lila." One night before bed she said to me, "You are my best friend."

A passing statement or not, it startled me. A parent was not supposed to be her child's best friend. Then I gave my daughter a kiss and tucked her in. When my father was little, he believed he would marry his mother when he grew up. While he always remembered the strength of that conviction and remained close to her, he married my mother and proved to be a good husband.

A few nights ago I had a dream. Jane, a friend of hers, and I were on a mountaintop. We emerged from a high, secret woods and began to ski down. Towards the bottom, instead of following the other two, I swerved onto another slope, intending to meet up with them in a moment. But on my

way to them, the snow-covered ground dropped perpendic-
ularly away without warning. Miles below at the base of the
drop I saw a flat, white surface stretching as far as an ocean.
I could not get to the girls. Panic may have awakened me
slightly, but the dream continued, although less vividly. I
was searching through empty hills. Then, I was in a mountain town, searching. A telephone appeared before me. I
would be able to communicate with my daughter.

32

On those days when I lie down for a while, usually in the late afternoon, and talk to my mother on the phone, I sometimes pull up a quilt she gave me for my birthday. It is light and machine washable. The underside is a pale yellow. The flowered or plain small squares on top are pastel shades. While all the blankets covering Bob's and my bed are thrown into a chest each morning, it stays on top of the bedspread. Even when I do not call, it comforts me, as if it were my mother's voice on the other end of the line.

Until I met Bob and had Jane, my mother was the most important person in my life. From an early age I realized her power over me but failed to see what I demanded in return: a perfect romantic heroine. Romanticizing the most important person in my life, as the fictitious Jo romanticized Marmee, I tended to romanticize others, like Stella, and to be romanticized in return. That led to my being controlled by what I thought others wanted me to be. And because of what I wanted them to be, I was too controlling. By my early twenties I seldom relaxed in the presence of the people in my life and made less effort to see them.

In my late twenties the effects of this scenario started me nipping at those who were to blame. My belated rebellion against my mother, whom I romanticized, was not as difficult as the one I waged against my sister Anne, inclined to romanticize me. It was easier to speak up to my mother. She listened to my allegations and read my accusatory letters, and her reply inevitably was, "I love you and always have."

During that brief hostile spell, I charged her with being too distant from her children and for not adequately attending to their emotional needs. The hug from my ten-year-old self, which she had refused during that fourth grade winter, symbolized the heart of my complaint. I knew her parents had raised her with more distance from them than she had extended to her own children, but until she was ten or eleven she had been the main charge of a beloved nanny, who had stayed on with the family through my mother's teen years.

After I reread *Little Women* as an adult, I read about the real Marmee, Abba May Alcott, who, like her fictional counterpart, raised four girls, Louisa May Alcott included. Unlike Marmee, Abba May seemed unable in the eyes of biographer May Sarton to let them go. If that family's intimacy, which I envied, was not fictitious, did it prevent the growth of its members later on? Sarton also underlined Marmee's words to Jo: "I am angry nearly every day of my life, Jo, but I have learned not to show it; and I still hope to learn not to feel it, though it may take me another forty years to do so."

If my mother gave too little attention to my emotional needs at various times when I was growing up, neither did she smother me with her own outlook or ambitions. She believed anger was a form of rudeness, if directed against a parent, and did not allow it. But she did not hide her own when we misbehaved, nor did she condemn it in general. When I, as an adult, presented her with mine, she did not say, "Learn not to show or feel it."

At the time of the hug during my first year at a new school, my mother made me a red wool skirt. She was proud of it, as she sewed slowly and rarely, but its style embarrassed me. Although I liked the color, and the skirt was skillfully made, I never wore it. Did I tell my mother it was lost? In the back of that large house was a hall lined with a few unused rooms, initially the maids' quarters. In one of the empty closets, I hung the skirt. I think of it hanging by itself, hidden and unworn, and I wonder how my mother would have felt had she found it there.

But my mother's guilt over the hug she did not return is far worse than mine over the skirt I did not wear: I was rejecting a piece of clothing, while she was rejecting me. Yet the skirt could equal many things my mother did for me that I failed to appreciate at the time: hiring a tutor when she discovered I could not read; teaching me how to play tennis; having photographs made of my artwork to send along in the form of a booklet with my college transfer application. When I came home from boarding school for my first break, she showed me a new skill she had learned in engraving. Oddly enough, I could tell from her hands, working on the block, how much she had missed me. I doubt if I responded in measure. So, if the skirt, like the hug, stands for more than itself, then the two are equal: each a different offering of love bespeaking a different expectation.

Even as I grew older, my expectations got in the way of my seeing my mother's own insecurity and depression. I tended to confuse them with lack of love for me. In fact, I used to regard whatever my mother said or did with the bias of being her daughter. Now I am able to give her more freedom to be herself, even as I am freer, and the pleasure of our time together is compounded.

My mother still regards her parents' distance from their children favorably: it gave her mother and father perspective. But it may have also contributed to her tendency to romanticize them, particularly her mother, a tendency which runs strong on both sides of my family. My father romanticized his mother; my grandparents theirs; my mother hers; I my mother. And the parents, again mostly the mothers, romanticized their children, or one or two or three of them, and still do, down to the present day. Even Jane and I, with less distance between us, struggle with that mutual tendency which governs and blinds us at times. So it may be something inherited and not all caused by parents seeing their children at relatively scarce, regulated, and convenient times of day. Or is it just a natural, mostly positive phenomenon between parents and children, one to which I am paying attention in order to know it better? For, if too pronounced, it may contribute to isolationist tendencies and to the social insecurity which in the long run and in my case has resulted in a growing inability to finish paintings.

Now, if my mother happens to remark to me how beneficial parents' distance from their children can be, I agree, then add with a smile, "But remember, you had Nanny."

33

I do not forget Jane's birthday because she reminds me of it far in advance. But the gifts I have given have sometimes disappointed her. One night before Christmas when she and I were walking Homer in the neighborhood, she remarked that she knew she was not going to get what she wanted.

"What do you want?"

"First, a dance costume like the one Jessica just got for her birthday."

"Not an ice skating costume?" I was surprised, as she had been saving for one throughout the fall and early winter, although she was still only halfway there.

"No. Second, a large, stuffed puppy. Third, some clothes for Baby, and fourth, some surprises."

Hearing the longing in her voice, I was silent. Material things matter to me, but I am wary of them. I seldom desire them the way Jane, Bob, and Anne do. Every Christmas, like a magician, Anne discovers what Jane wants most and seems to pull it out of the big hat she wears for the beauty and extension of herself. That is how she looks upon possessions in general, while I tend to regard them as walls which obscure. When I was seventeen, my father gave me a Volvo of my own to drive to college. As much as I grew to love it, when he presented it to me, I hid my disappointment. I wanted a Volkswagen, a small, inconspicuous car that would not draw away from the person I was.

Shortly before I graduated from college, my father died. Our house, with its size, elegance, and formality, which he in particular loved, seemed to lose its center. My mother put it on the market. Between the couple of months it took to sell and for my mother to buy a smaller house, possessions, big and little, costly and cheap, ruled us. At times, their endless sorting, packing, and departure helped to distract my mother from her grief. Then again, their sentimental value intensified it.

When my mother left home to live with my father on Flamingo, for two decades her principal residence was relatively modest, and her surrounding possessions were few. In the fall after my father died, I left my wealthy home town for the city and resided for the next decade in two one-room apartments. The one-rooms were in keeping with what I could afford, and I did not long for better quarters. When I

met Bob, I was living in a third, bigger space with a hall, living room, bedroom, and kitchen, but the building and area were still somewhat rundown and insecure.

After we moved into our present condominium apartment with its comparative safety and spaciousness, for a while I had a recurring dream of returning to those past rooms and of their being empty except for myself. I would awaken frightened. For over thirteen years until I met Bob, I wanted love and happiness with an intensity the dream revealed. It emphasized the emptiness of the rooms in juxtaposition with the intensity of my longing when I lived in them. What I feared was a return to the loneliness that filled them up, not the spaces themselves or their lack of physical possessions.

Although I am writing this book in order to finish paintings, the ensuing search seems to be influencing a more fractured longing: to be a good wife, mother, daughter, sibling, friend, writer, painter. But that night close to Christmas, Jane longed for things, specific things. I looked at my heroine and saw a difference between us of approach involving surfaces versus depths. Here she resembled Anne and Bob, not me. But the force of her desires I equated with my own, and suddenly it seemed important that she get what she wanted for Christmas, not what she said she wanted when the ice skating costume seemed out of reach. Reflecting upon my Puritan nature, I was grateful she had Anne as a benefactor.

Because his parents are not living or because the gifts he has received over the years have dulled his expectations or for some other reason, Bob has to struggle to find the Christmas spirit. When Jane was let down by the few presents she chose to open on Christmas Eve, he took her to the roof to look above the tree tops and city lights for Santa's sleigh.

There in the high, cold darkness the two were looking for a sleigh carrying gifts, but what they saw were the stars.

Were they so different from me after all? Did the surfaces they chose to focus on signify the same depths that governed me? Could either of them have been the child that bicycled to the lighthouse?

Jane began to doubt Santa Claus as early as last fall, but late that night before Christmas she woke to hear a "ho ho" in the dining room where he was drinking the milk and eating the cookies she had set out for him. The next morning she believed in him for one last season. His gifts and the others she received were what she wanted, particularly the ice skating costume. Anne's daughter, a skater, had picked it out and sent it after Anne called us long distance and inquired about Jane's activities.

After wearing it to class a few times, Jane loaned it first to Jessica, then to Ravenna. For her birthday in February she received from Lynn, Bob's oldest sister, an ice skating costume made to order. In May, Jessica, Jane, and I stopped at a yard sale where Jane picked out a pink apron with metallic circles dangling on its front. The woman running the sale said the apron was part of a costume her daughter had worn when she was a penguin on skates. When I told her Jane and Jessica skated too, she disappeared into the house and returned with four complete outfits as beautiful as any in the ice skating apparel shop. "You may have each for a dollar," she said. Jessica chose first, as she did not own any, and Jane took the other three.

By coincidence, Lynn was coming to dinner that night. Jane could not wait to show off her collection. "I don't know," Bob said to me, worried that his sister might feel her expensive birthday gift was now redundant. "Maybe Jane shouldn't mention the others."

I had been worrying along those lines too but said, "I've spent a lot of energy in my life hiding things: where I come from, what I have, what I don't have, what I want, what I am. I don't want Jane to start doing the same thing."

On Bob's and my bed Jane laid out all the glistening materials and colors: gold, pale pink, purple, red and white, black with neon strips. Then Lynn came with a box under her arm containing a new ice skating outfit she had not been able to resist buying for her niece.

The last apartment I lived in by myself, the largest one, overlooked the drive — on whose center strip my elderly neighbors congregated — and the park beyond. In summer the flat, sandy area directly across from my window was occasionally used for local ball games or a traveling amusement show which would settle in for a number of nights, maybe even for a week or longer, with its ferris wheel, merry-go-round, food booths, and games. The rest of the time the area was usually empty of people.

One hot, quiet mid-afternoon I was working on a drawing when from somewhere within the leafy depths lining that stretch came the beat of a drum. On and on it went. It seemed to sum up a decade of solitary living in the pursuit of something which offered few tangible rewards. The drummer could not know I was listening or know how that magic beat suspended time for me and helped keep me from wondering too much about what I was missing, like clothes or ice skating outfits; or how it evoked not the many viewers I was acquainted with who doubted what I did, but others, unknown to me, who, standing before a painting I had declared finished and perfect, agreed.

Another time I was in Scotland and working on a watercolor upstairs in my room during a visit to the ancestral summer home of Anne's husband. Anne was down in the mud room cleaning a gun and whistling. The sound carried up to me in prolonged variations and repetitions like the drumming but different. The place in Scotland is to Anne what Lupin, seldom visited by her, is to me. And her whistling—a crazy, almost painful expression of happiness—amazed but discomforted me because, unlike the drummer's music, its single-noted, frenetic pluralism negated the narrower focus of my world.

34

Like her whistling, Anne's presents to me over the years have at times caused discomfort, even as they may have opened my eyes to something new. The extravagance and variety of them—even of the smallest things—tended to proclaim her outlook and cancel out mine. When a Christmas tree arrived on the doorstep of my first apartment, my own decorations seemed insignificant and that live, sweet-smelling, green, green mass of needles filled and obliterated the small space.

The Christmas before last she gave Jane an aquarium, calling first to see if I minded, since it would involve some work on my part. I guardedly acquiesced. Although smaller than the tree, the fish and their domain invaded our place just as insidiously, but this time I took up the challenge—as Jane and Bob were not interested—and over the past year and a half the gift has duly instructed me about the underwater world.

One Saturday this spring, recovering from a cold I had just caught, Jane asked to have a friend over. Not feeling quite well, she called Cary first, then Lila. Both were away. Only then did she call Caitlin, a friend from her closest nucleus of friends but an independent child whose interests were not always the same as her own. Caitlin had a cold too, so her parents did not object to leaving her with us that unseasonably hot afternoon. As always before a visit from Caitlin, Jane had planned an activity.

To prevent the window light from promoting algae in the fish tank, I had finally covered its back and two exposed sides with white paper which I had hoped Jane would decorate with fish murals. As Caitlin liked to draw, that was Jane's idea of something to do with her.

"Afterwards, if you like, I'll take you to the park," I offered reluctantly, feeling unwell and sluggish from my cold and the heat. As Bob was away for the day, I could not call upon him.

The girls worked for about an hour, sitting on the floor with their paper on two of the low living room window sills. What breezes there were blew past them through the room and out the opposing dining room windows, so they had chosen the coolest spot in the condominium. After stopping for milk and cookies, they worked a while longer before disappearing into Jane's room, leaving behind their aquatic drawings. I taped the sheets back onto the aquarium's sides and watched the fish swim against their new background of whales, seals, sea horses, sea grass, and schools of fish.

Until about a month ago, my interest in the tank grew into an obsession. It was to be a perfect world I controlled. I bought exotic fish and plants and set a glass bottle into the pebbles lining the bottom. The reflecting angles of the tank's uncovered sides added mystery and depth to the water. Little flashes of color circled about and zapped food from the surface.

Although I frequently tested the water, one by one the fish stopped eating and died. The plants were nibbled at and clogged the filter. The electric light they required promoted algae, which eventually covered the objects in the tank, spotted the glass sides, and floated in the water itself, obscuring all. I scrubbed the tank clean, exchanged a proportion of old water for new, bought more fish, and put in different plants. Everything was perfect again.

Finally, I threw out the plants, turned off the light, taped paper to three sides of the tank, stopped replacing the fish, and left a ceramic log, not beautiful but easy to clean, in the bottom center. Now in the ten gallons of water swim four tiny survivors: three glow-lights and one neon tetra. I observe them with pleasure but rarely change their water or clean the tank. It looks all right. There is only a little algae growing in the corners.

I lost interest in the project not because of my failures but because I realized that although I might be on the right track I was going the wrong direction. The aquarium represented an effort towards more control, whereas this book, which eventually replaced it, was about letting go. Even as I started to write about it, I was forced to let go, taking my chances at wasting a morning. What did the aquarium have to do with anything, I asked myself, but kept writing.

I watched the fish until the children returned to the living room. They wanted to go to the park, but it had begun to rain. Automatically, I said no. Colds and rain did not mix.

After reminding me a few times of my promise to take them, Jane picked up a plastic lid lying nearby and threw it in my direction. It hit my face, and I said, "No friend tomorrow." I retreated to my bedroom and lay down.

We had three umbrellas. I had presumed the children would quickly abandon theirs and get themselves soaked. If Caitlin's cold grew worse, her parents might blame her walk in the rain. But at the time I neglected to ask myself if my reply could have been yes.

I recalled the fear in Jane's eyes when the lid hit me and how, growing up, I had modified my behavior to avoid spankings. Except for my giving Jane an involuntary slap on her clothed behind three or four times in her life, I have never spanked her. Neither has Bob. We agree with the general thinking of the day that physical force is not a good way to manage children. Yet, although our way of handling Jane is less humiliating than my parents' for the kind of child I was, it is over less quickly.

If Jane has a child, she may consider punishment detrimental to a sense of self-respect, just as many parents today scoff at spanking. Praise versus lack of praise may be more the mode.

When I plagiarized the French sentences, the school sent me home for the weekend: a treat during my boarding school years and inappropriate as punishment. More likely, I was supposed to think things over and discuss them with my parents. My shame was such, I could do neither.

Upon my return to school, the headmistress, whose good opinion I had courted from the beginning, seemed no longer interested in me. My advisor mentioned her disappointment and exhibited distrust of my past work. My French teacher avoided me.

Upon correcting my homework, she had gone to my room—after sending my two roommates away and arousing their suspicions concerning the trouble I was in—found the book on top of my desk with the sentences on its back cover, gone directly to my advisor, and then to the headmistress. Her silence, my advisor's lack of faith, and the headmistress' withdrawal were my punishments. For the rest of the day after the crime was discovered, a sense of the world's condemnation flooded my adolescent mind. I never mentioned the incident to anyone.

The next morning during school assembly I was scheduled to accompany the violin teacher and one of his students. From a young age, when my aunt taught us girls how to play, the piano had been a solace to me. That the others were better did not phase me. In fact, when my sisters left home for good and I was a senior at high school, I stopped taking lessons and rarely played.

Being part of a trio—the only time I accompanied other players—was a musical high for me. My part was relatively simple, but I was playing pieces I liked with good musicians. At the recital before touching the keyboard, I looked at the audience of waiting faces: it was innocent; I was not. The students did not know what I had done, but I was sure the teachers did. By the end of the performance the invisible wall had come down.

I have returned to the school every now and then with gratitude rather than anger. In many other respects it gave of itself generously and wisely. Even its treatment of my mistake was kinder than other schools might have been at the time, neither expelling nor humiliating me before others by making my behavior public. Later, the headmistress wrote a recommendation that played a major part in helping me transfer to the college of my choice.

Lying on my bed, I returned to mulling over Jane's smaller mistake. I thought of her expression when the lid hit me: her own loss of control seemed to have scared her more than the lost privilege did. While I was teaching myself about less control, I had to teach her about more without making fear a common bond between us.

Slowly, I moved to get up. In the dining room the girls presented me with a banana on a plate. It was peeled and split down the middle and filled with cut-up pieces of apple, grape, and plum.

The rain finally stopped, and we had time to take Homer for a short walk in the neighborhood before driving Caitlin home. Caitlin ran ahead with Homer on a leash, while Jane, upset about no friend the next day, argued at my side. Then she caught up to her friend with the idea of shaking the leaves' wetness onto their heads. The girls sought out bushes and low branches of trees, and soon they were as wet as if they had been out in the rainstorm.

Sunday morning, Caitlin called to see if Jane could come over and play. I wavered, then recalled Jane as a baby hanging by her hands from her crib's railing, refusing to lie down even in the last stages of exhaustion. Worried that the stubbornness her anger and hurt provoked then could turn destructive, I said no. Jane was upset all over again, but Bob agreed with me, and we stood firm.

I suspected that Caitlin asked Jane over in part to see if my ruling of the day before would be carried out. I smiled faintly.

This chapter has left a jumble of impressions in my mind accompanied by a deeper sense of my fallibilities as an artist: Anne's fish tank ending up with the children's sea drawings and the sparse inhabitants and the green algae in the corners, all signifying a less controlled but more perfect world than the one I had originally envisioned; my inept French homework, dull except for what I had taken from somebody else. I had nothing to say because I could not recognize truth as something messy, changeable, and imperfect. During the recital I played before the world and how badly or well did not matter, only what I wanted to convey through the music: an overriding desire to belong?

Finally, there is the decision I made on Sunday: no to Jane going over to Caitlin's house. And the ones made on Saturday: no to walking in the rain; no to my own disinclination to walk at all; and yes to letting the girls get wet in the sunshine. Towards the end of a painting, when it is close to being frozen in time, different ways of looking at what I have done multiply in my mind and overwhelm my efforts. In sudden doubt and frustration I paint over an entire canvas rather than wait until I am calmer and can say no to that, no to this, and yes to that.

35

Late this spring towards the end of second grade Jane had an idea: she and her friends would put on a circus for the parents. The school playground, empty after school hours, seemed a good place for it, offering bars for gymnastics and tricks. Jane's friends were enthusiastic about the idea.

One afternoon when I came to pick her up from school, I found Jane in the playground reviewing each act and carefully writing down its heading and sequence of appearance. As I watched, I thought how things had changed in a year, how well the girls worked together, how sure Jane was, and how supportive Jessica was of an idea not her own.

The big evening arrived. We parents sat on the bleachers. Jane had given us each a paper ticket with a seat number on it. Lila had made a large collage which spelled out CIRCUS. Cary's mother had found some bright-colored hula hoops. Provided by us parents and laid out on a special part of the bleachers were peanut butter and jelly sandwiches, potato chips, watermelon, and six boxes of circus crackers, one for each child. Unfortunately, Jessica was away on a trip with her family, and Caitlin was at a best friend's birthday party. The costumes were an assortment from Jane's ice skating, Cary's dress-up, and Lila's ballet outfits. Jane announced the show under Lila's circus sign. Cary did her hula hoop act. Beatrice and Jane did gymnastics in unison on a bar. Lila pointed and dipped and rose on a ladder. Ravenna did a split and some bar tricks, and Tashime, hanging with a bar under one knee, circled over and under repeatedly. Then the girls lined up and bowed to the applause.

I wanted to freeze those six smiling faces into my memory. Little by little during the second grade the girls had grown socially until they had reached this milestone of cooperation.

36

Almost a year and a half has passed since I began this book. Last summer in Maine I worked on what I had written instead of painting. During the winter and early spring months of Jane's third grade year, I wrote further. Then I put the book away on the shelf under my desk.

Just as I was beginning to paint again, I noticed Bob battling an old obsession: to travel. I stopped work and called a friend in Paris. She and her family would be away during Jane's spring vacation, but we could stay in their condominium.

Paris was cold, gray, and damp. Our first moments off the plane alarmed Bob and me because our traveling pecking order seemed reversed. On our first and subsequent trips to Italy Bob was the guide, but, unlike me, he had not studied French. It did not seem to reassure either of us that he was fluent in Italian, while my French, always poor in school, was mostly forgotten.

Upon our arrival at our building, Bob caught his thumb in the heavy entry door. It swelled and throbbed, intruding upon his sleep for a few nights. Also, he was unprepared for both the weather and Jane's reluctance to go along with anything he wanted to do. The second day a crisis peaked before lunch. Bob wanted to eat in a bistro, Jane in the condominium apartment, and I, because it was cheaper, in the park. The bistro won out but twenty-four hours later we were consuming baguettes in chilly outdoor air. For the rest of the trip we split up during the day, Bob and I taking turns with Jane.

On Lupin Bob comes closest to happiness. There, in a favorite setting, life passes him by less than in other places, especially as friends visit on weekends. In Paris his discontent threatened to overwhelm him. The world he wanted was close by but economically not viable. Italy was only a drive away, Paris restaurants around the corner. He wanted to see things from early morning to late at night and not alone or with a reluctant nine-year-old in tow.

Yet he was the one who provided Jane with the highlight of her trip. One of her school assignments was to keep a diary. Every night she wrote a couple of perfunctory lines except for the page and a half that marked the day Bob took her to an amusement park in the Bois de Boulogne, just as his uncle had taken him years ago to Coney Island.

For most of the vacation, however, he was withdrawn, inwardly chaffing against the conditions of the trip. I did not mind sleeping late with Jane and spending five or so hours a day out in the city. A walk along the Seine, a ride on a bus with its clean windows and interior, a park, and always the foreign, elegant residence awaiting our return. I wanted some critical—but not necessarily long—hours in museums. But on my own I did not object to seeing Paris more from Jane's eyes. Soon, she would be grown up. "Soon, I will be old," Bob said. It flashed across our minds for the first time: how were we going to cope with the responsibility of a child for all the years ahead?

The afternoon before we left Paris, Jane and I had a fight in the Champs de Mars near our building. It centered around what we were going to do for the next few hours. Egged on more by Bob's discontent than my own, when Jane refused to go along with my plans for the day, I called her a nuisance and expressed regret at bringing her on the trip. She wandered off into the park. From my distant bench near the bus stop where our argument began, I kept an eye on her. I thought about children who ran away from home and about my mother who felt the weight of her ten-year-old's hug. For the second time within a week and since Jane's birth, doubts concerning my stamina as a parent besieged me.

I sat frozen on the bench. Jane came closer and climbed to the top of a stone slide marking the park's entrance. I went over and sat at the bottom of it. She slid down and gave me a kiss. She suggested that instead of making me take her to le Bon Marché, the well-known department store two bus rides away, we go to a wagon she had spotted in the park.

Since she was interested in clothes, I had initially suggested we see the temporary costume exhibit at the Louvre. Unrealized by either of us until that moment, she did not want to go to Le Bon Marché any more than I did the Louvre. The park and wagon were what we wanted.

The wagon was set by itself on the far side of the park. The vendor was from Africa, and her wares consisted of scarves, bags, and tourist trinkets. Before she picked out what to buy with her francs, Jane spent a long time examining everything. I relaxed on a nearby bench, sharing her delight in the quiet, unordered time. The air was warmer than it had been since our arrival, and the early spring sun blazed behind transparent clouds.

37

One afternoon towards the middle of our stay in Paris, Bob and Jane left me at the Musée d'Orsay. I started at the top floor and slowly made my way down, discouraged by my lack of interest. On the second floor I paused in front of a large, white bas-relief sculpture. I looked at it idly; it had nothing to do with me or my work. A dramatic piece, it consisted of three men on the face of a cliff. On the lower ledge an eagle lay dead with an arrow through its back. One wing hung over the waist-high pedestal. Crouching next to the dead bird, the bearer of the arrows looked up at his two companions. They were fighting what was apparently the eagle's mate and were in danger of being pushed off the cliff. I studied the men and eagles for a long time.

The unexpected appeal of that relatively traditional piece led me to the Louvre a few days later. Again, I was bored until a large painting depicting Napoleon amid the aftermath of one of his battles drew my attention. Later, at the end of a long corridor among fifteenth century work, I found a painting I vaguely remembered from an art history course.

A husband and wife were sitting side by side. The wife, holding an open Bible or some spiritual book in her hands, was glancing reluctantly over at the focus of her husband's attention: gold coins and jewelry. Another kind of battle was going on, centuries old but close to home.

Our splitting up on account of Jane's resistance to sightseeing contributed to Bob's frustration. But on another level, instead of our usual skirmishes, he and I were fighting a war.

Over what? Spiritualism versus materialism, as suggested in the painting? Not really. Something else: money. How much should be saved; how much spent; and on what. "Make some money," says Bob, who knows how; "Save," say I, knowing how.

Next came a portrait by the same artist of a mother and child, maybe Jane and me when she was a toddler. It too might have taught me something, but I passed it with only a glance. What I had been looking for since arriving in Paris, I had found.

About an hour after Bob and Jane left me that afternoon at the Musée D'Orsay, I realized that our only key to the condominium was in my purse. Grateful for what I had seen, I was not too disappointed to leave. But when I opened the door on our deserted place filled with momentary late after-noon sun, I regretted that my adventures for the day had to end so early. The concierge, who was usually out during the afternoon, knocked. She had let my husband and daughter in earlier and given them a spare key, to be returned in the evening. After she departed, I paused before the door. Had I understood her correctly? Should I stay and welcome Bob and Jane back? As if swimming against a current, I left.

Earlier, on the return bus ride from the museum, I listened to two Americans speaking French. One told the other, if she saw nothing else in Paris, she should see the Luxembourg Gardens. The speaker had lived for the past two years in Paris, teaching English. This much I understood from her French, which was clearer to me than the native accent. The friend replied that the gardens would have to wait; she was leaving the next day.

"Il faut les voir maintenant," the first speaker said, urging her friend to see them now.

"Bonjour, Monsieur. Les Jardins de Luxembourg, s'il vous plaît?" I inquired timidly of the bus driver that late after-noon, having left my map at the condominium.

"Uni," I thought he replied. I searched the bus route posted above for a stop that sounded like Uni. Cluny, I found, and eventually I disembarked onto a busy street.

"Bonjour, Madame, où sont les Jardins de Luxembourg?" I asked a passing elderly woman.

She smiled at me and replied, "Tout droit."

I continued straight ahead until I reached the park's entrance. It had turned into a somber, chilly late afternoon with only a few people on the grounds, but here and there a policeman stood formally at his post. To one side, evening shadows advanced under trees closely spaced and well cared for with bottom branches forming a flat, low ceiling. Before me, contained by its steely lines, was a central pool. The fish within, big for pool fish and gray not gold, moved slowly about in clean water which just covered them. A grave, palatial building overlooked the pool. I walked under the trees and came across a group of miniature horses being led off somewhere at the end of the day.

After a visit of about half an hour, I headed back, this time asking more easily of a man at the bus stop where I could

catch the number eighty-seven bus going in the opposite direction. Bob and Jane greeted me with supper made and no complaints concerning my absence. I slept badly.

Insomnia plagued most of my visit in Paris but especially after hours alone in the city. Not having suffered from it to such a degree since before I married, I believed its presence was due primarily to Bob's withdrawn state but also to something else. On our past trips to Italy, I had followed Bob around, enjoying his expertise as a guide but more interested in getting to know him than Italy or myself. In Paris I recognized no central focus for my sightseeing. This lack by itself provoked unease.

Yet without it I might have missed the bas-relief sculpture; Napoleon's battlefield; the fifteenth century couple; the conversation—one I would not have made an effort to understand—which inspired my getting to and from the Luxembourg Gardens; and the realization that the conversation, the leaving, the finding, and the returning were no less important than the gardens.

On this trip I needed to discover for myself what I was to take home, but it came to me later that Bob's outlook during our travels together, similar to his general outlook but more apparent and less complicated, had already rubbed off on me in some measure and had made my approach to Paris' surfaces more successful.

"How was Paris?" my friends and acquaintances asked when I returned. "What did you see?"

I might have answered, "I saw some paintings and a sculpture. I saw the Luxembourg Gardens and three French people who gave me directions. I saw two Algerians, one who sold tourist trinkets to Jane and another who wrapped some strands of her hair for twenty francs. And I saw the Seine."

38

Our place in Paris was near the Seine. My hours with Jane were divided between the condominium apartment, where she wanted to be, and the river, my preference. The river was yellow and swollen and turbulent during our stay. One day Jane remarked that sometimes she felt like a duck, as if she could jump into the water. I said people felt that way sometimes, including myself. Thank goodness, there was usually a big distance between such thought and action. We were walking along the lower path directly next to the water, and I imagined Jane caught in its opaque rush.

"What would you do if I fell in?" she asked idly.

"Jump in after you, of course," I said. But the river was different from the still water of the island pond where I had attempted to rescue my younger brother. And my father was not here to pull us out.

Spanning a natural inlet on Flamingo far from town was a pump. It drew the ocean into a canal which ran inland. Gradually, the canal's sides narrowed, and the depth and force of the flow lessened until, by the time it reached the holding reservoir, it barely moved. There, under hot sun and dry wind it evaporated into a brinier mixture before sliding through gates into individual pans.

The gates were briny boards set into vertical wooden slots which my father at odd hours, sometimes driving out from town to do so, regulated with a pick ax. Once inside the pans, the saturated mass gradually turned a rich pink.

We children would go a little distance from the pump and jump into the canal. At first we would tumble with a current impossible to fight. It would push us down, turn us over, separate us, and throw us together before it became a steadier force. Still, we could not swim against it, only float and turn while propelled forward. Then we could swim, just barely, and at last easily. At that point, we would climb up the low, stony incline, run back a short distance from the pump, and jump again.

Flying home from Paris these many years later, I equated swimming at the pump with the few times I had been free among other people. If my life up until now had been a struggle for control, in the future I might learn how to let go more: of myself, my work, of Bob, Jane, and my mother.

Paris emphasized the imbalance, less extreme at home but present, between Bob's and my time with Jane and our time together. Since Jane's birth, I had worried about it but thought it necessary. During the past year I worried about it more but made no changes. Now, maybe I could, and, the next time I needed to, I might be able to separate from Bob more easily without apprehension engulfing me in the form of sleeplessness.

Some of the truth I have found concerning our trip was this: we visited Paris because my friends lent us their condominium. I called my friends because of Bob. I would not have called them for myself. For him, I let go my preferred routine. Indirectly, he moved me forward and, by doing so, taught me, not so much about our differences but how we were the same.

In the past I have feared recognition of our sameness, depending, as I thought I did, upon Bob for qualities other than mine. Now the part of me that used to fall in love with the romanticized unknown in the other sex, thinking it would break through my control and free me from myself, has vanished. "Know thyself" has taken its place, followed by "The truth shall set you free."

On the other hand, I might have encouraged Bob to pause more often in order to create resting spots of meaning along the way. I might have said to him, "I came to Paris for you. For the duration of this trip, try to find happiness within the means I feel comfortable with. Let go of the rest."

Coming home to the brown, shallow river of our small city, we had passed a family crisis. For the few days that remained until school started again, Jane played in her room and drew and read. She made few demands upon us. Bob shared with her the paraphernalia he had saved from Paris— museum ticket stubs, coins, postcards, maps — and each made a collage.

I vacuumed the apartment and swept out my studio. Another trip completed, as important as the one Bob and I took to Italy before we were married. That was all closeness between us with Jane glimpsed in a dream but as yet unborn. The darkness of Assisi was only a small part of the whole. But Paris, beautiful and threatening like my dreams, was lonely, except for the times when I was by myself or with Jane; Bob was the distant one. Yet in the same way spring brought about the turbulence of the Seine, a different kind of spring motivated Bob's and my struggle in Paris. Like the Seine from its urban stone walls, even if the truth we found recedes from our minds, it will leave its mark upon us.

39

Upon our return from Paris I stretched some canvases. An idea of what to paint on the next one came to mind as soon as I had set down—in one dry coat of paint—an idea on the preceding one. The canvases stood as high as my waist or higher. All contained only one or two objects: a china flamingo against a mirror; a lamp and trophy. Almost illustrative, they were inspired by what I saw rather than set up.

"You should paint your daughter, someone you care about, instead of still life." Two years ago the gallery director's advice proved to me her lack of comprehension regarding my work. I missed its overall shading of truth. Later, I painted a horse, a harbinger of what I was now painting, into a still life. And I started to write a book about Jane, which has turned into being about me.

During a visit to my studio in June Amy glanced with surprise at the backs of the large canvases stacked one behind the other, leaning against a wall. I reluctantly turned them around, then smiled at her reaction. Interest lit up her face as she looked. "You've made a leap," she said.

The canvases face the wall again, unfinished. Meanwhile, I have gone back to my old work and methods, filling in the empty spaces with objects, or replacing the objects with others, or removing many of the replaced objects in order to regain the empty spaces.

Again, I am caught up in the familiar, even at times, happy process of searching. It crosses my mind that the problem is less process than lack of faith. As the former evolves, it may become easier. And different approaches will help.

40

I am working again on the white bowl painting.

I remove the horse from behind the stick.

I remove the cup and bottle.

I sketch in a glass vase where the cup was.

The canvas' edge does not eliminate part of the vase as it did the cup, and the vase's bubbled surface, even in its unfinished state, picks up and repeats the theme of the bracelet's plastic balls. A bottle no longer cuts the bowl's base in two. The stick, without the horse behind it, balances free on top of the rock, barely touching its highest curve. Things connect, rather than intersect, through shape, reflection, or color. The horse is gone, but there will be another painting for it.

"When I finish the vase, this painting will be done," I tell myself. But my interest has gone. A good disciplinarian, I mix the turquoise color, but then I stop, rinse the brush, take the painting from the easel, and put another in its place.

In the late fall of Jane's fifth grade year I exchange the vase for a purple flashlight turned towards the viewer. It is not on, but a few strokes of white paint, thicker and looser than elsewhere, emanate from its bulb like two rays from a barely visible moon. But where is the moon's night? A week later I put in the black cloth again, this time not as a small mirrored rectangle on a distant wall but enlarged and immediate, filling the background. The embroidered flowers and leaves jump out of the blackness and pass in a brilliant row directly behind the bowl and its muted geometric pattern.

The background is the moon's night but also darkness bearing flowers. Done.

Sometime later, as if sleepwalking, I take the painting off my studio wall and add a baby's toy in front of the bowl. It stands right on the edge of the canvas, its red rim blatantly matching the red of the flowers on the cloth and encircling a floating duck. Finally, I paint a piece of coral leaning against the cloth, standing on end, its arms waving against the flowers. It is too flat and big for the painting, too white for its background position. It is perfect. Done, done, done.

The next summer I paint over most of a still life, leaving only the overall shape of a metal bird on a green table cloth. I stop and decide the painting is finished. The dark gray of the bird is hardly distinguishable from that of the green background surrounding and mixed into it. One rainy day on Lupin I had watched a bird move against a piece of bush and lawn. I take home the reworked, framed canvas and hang it in our dining room.

Bob and Jane dislike it, but one day a friend, who is grieving, sees it from the corner of her eye and asks, surprised and as if for an instant solaced, "Who painted that?" I look at the painting. Did I?

During Jane's seventh grade year I complete a canvas with a doll's wooden rocking chair, its color merging into the foreground, making it seem farther back than the dark, upright catalog in the distance. On the left edge of the canvas, nearer the catalog than the chair, is a china rabbit.

In the winter of Jane's eighth grade year I notice a decorated glass cup standing on a table in the sun. I finish painting it within three or four days, making a few technical corrections at a later date.

Then I start working on one of the large canvases, adding object after object, a collection of all the objects I have buried under paint over the years. In my happiness, it seems as if no effort—past, present, or future—is truly lost. I paint carefully, slowly, sometimes in the morning or afternoon or at odd hours here and there. Or I read a book in the studio instead of painting. I feel as free as that college classmate appeared to be with her large brush and sure, broad movements. Over the summer I do not look at it. During the week before Open Studios, I paint over some of the objects and work on others. In the couple of hours before opening time I make a last touch, then another, and then for two days, as the viewers come and go, I marvel at my finished painting.

The dictionary defines epiglottis as the thin cartilaginous structure. Folding over the glottis, the vocal apparatus of the larynx, it keeps food and liquid from the trachea, which carries air to the lungs. The optic nerve does not threaten breathing but is closer to the brain. Directly behind it is a spool of tape with pictures imprinted instead of words. It has a free end to be pinched and gently pulled out of the eye without dislodging its intricate surroundings.

In the fall of Jane's sixth grade year a critic from a contemporary art monthly reviews the Open Studios in my district and focuses on the work of three artists, including mine, to praise. That winter a gallery returns my slides without comment. The following year I get a painting accepted into a juried show subsequently panned in a local newspaper, and Amy brings her college art student majors for a studio visit.

41

In the past more than a few people at a social event would make me nervous. Too many feelings to try and please; too many conflicting demands sensed. To whom should I talk? Where should I sit? Like Homer, nervously wagging his tail when he entered a room of acquaintances or unknown people, I would smile in alarm, even as I remembered my grandmother firmly and uncharacteristically advising me, as if she were stating a hard-learned lesson: "You can't please everyone."

One weekend, shortly after Jane graduated from third grade, I found myself having fun with a group of people— mostly acquaintances. When I was not enjoying the details, I was forgiving of them or felt forgiven: sitting where I wanted to or where I did not; talking to those I chose or to whom chose me about subjects that were superficial or weighty or in-between.

After that weekend we left for our three weeks in Maine. One afternoon I lost my way in the woods and became caught up to my waist in the brambles of raspberry bushes. My feet were slipping on overturned, rotting tree trunks and fallen branches and into the gaps between. I stopped for a moment and looked up at blue sky and encircling spruce that cut off the wind. I imagined myself over a year ago in the same situation and how uneasy I would have been. Eventually, finding my way back, even the big house looked different, threatening less to obscure than being part of me and of the surrounding nature and of the first generation that had created it and of the present ones trying to maintain it and themselves as a family.

Today, when a heat wave keeps me from my studio, I take the cardboard box from under my desk to the city library and begin to look the manuscript over. Thinking upon those two times when I felt free, I understand that something is finished. What I wrote during the past winter and early spring—all that followed the circus at the end of Jane's second grade year—was not an endless adding on but instead a completed stage of a process as tedious and fulfilling in the long run as the way I paint.

At the peak of midsummer's heat, I settle down to read what I began writing during the preceding, coldest months of the year.

42

A Friday, hot and damp, was Jane's last day of second grade, since we were off to Maine before the others got out on Monday. After school was over, the teacher came to tea, an event long planned and awaited by Jane, who showed her around. Then we had cold drinks and fruit and cake. Halfway through, Jane changed into a bathing suit, filled a small plastic tub and cooking pot with water, and placed them in the kitchen doorway. She sat in the tub, put her feet in the pot, and smiled broadly at the grownups talking around the dining room table. When saying good-bye, the teacher put her arm around her and kissed her, but by then the day's excitement had overtaken Jane. She did not seem to notice the affectionate gesture. Before bed, she asked if I would bring her to school Monday at the regular time, just before our scheduled departure for Lupin.

Monday morning, despite the rush to get off, I took her to school and waited patiently in the car while she disappeared into the building. If I had to pick exactly when her early childhood ended, I would choose the moment when, her good-byes completed, she ran back towards the waiting car. It coincided with an overall feeling of closure on my part regarding her first eight years. But my book is still unfinished seven months later, and a sense of where it is going eludes me. So I continue to write, hoping some landmarks will appear.

Last summer, Jane read to herself as well as listened to me. Unlike the previous fall, on the first day of third grade she was not behind in reading. Late in the summer, I had begun to read an adult nonfiction book here and there to myself, but my reading of fiction was still anchored at Jane's level, although it seemed as if her taste was branching away from my own and centering more on mysteries like the Nancy Drew and Box Car Children series. These I did not enjoy to the degree Jane did. I assumed a bond between us from her early childhood was disappearing.

Some days I did not read aloud to her at all, but before she went to bed, we read in the same room, each with our own book. Then I was surprised to recall that at the age of two, Jane's favorite book was a mystery: *The Supermarket Mystery*. I was mistaken to think her taste was only recently changing. Was I blind about other, more significant things during my years as a perfect mother?

As for third grade itself, in the fall Jane seemed changed: angrier and more ambivalent. Even her teacher, whom Jane likes, is not regarded as unequivocally as those before. Her first semester report card distressed her as much as it had the year before, but not because it included a couple of S pluses. Instead, she was upset by the teacher's comment:

> *She places a great deal of effort into her work. She works well in group situations. She is always kind and thoughtful of others.*

"All my teachers say the same thing," Jane said. She made me look up her report cards since kindergarten. She was right. Complimentary as the descriptions of her were, she wanted to be measured accurately. Her recent winter grades were all G's again, but what pleased her was the teacher's summing up:

> *She is able to listen to and weigh the merits of others' ideas and opinions. She expresses her own thoughts with clarity and confidence.*

A few days after school started Jane's new ambivalence surfaced in another area when I questioned her regarding her class section versus the one next door. She was quiet a moment before stating flatly, "It doesn't matter. I'm sick of everybody." She proceeded to see fewer friends than before, but the time she spent with them seemed more significant.

Ravenna, who lives just down the street from us, remains a close pal. Stella and I, for the time being, have let go of the possibility of a friendship outside the two girls. Except for a formal social occasion now and then, Stella has joined the parent ring of Jane and her friends. We guardians do not see each other as often as before because our children are at a less demanding age. But if our support is less palpable than during our children's earlier years, it is still there, ready to be called upon when needed.

Another change that has occurred is the decline, most likely temporary, of sleepovers. Starting last summer Jane would eagerly accept an invitation, only to call us around eleven to say good-night and suddenly ask for a ride home, often to the surprise of her friend, the parents, and herself. Eventually, I heard from the others that their daughters also had grown uncertain about spending the night away from home.

In the changing ebb and flow of friendships encouraged by new class sections each year, the groupings within Jane's closest circle vary slightly. Even outside school, the girls seem to play more with those friends who are in their own section. As more of Jane's friends are in the other classroom this year, once or twice she has felt left out. This is another change from second grade. And yet another is that I have begun to interfere more when social problems arise.

One evening before a midweek day off from school, Jane called around to see if anyone could come to her class at the local museum. Cary, who accompanied her there once

a week, was visiting her grandmother. Jane found her next
choices either away or doing
something with each other. She
angrily informed me of the situation,
adding that Lila was spending
the day at Ravenna's house. As
a rule, she was not possessive.
But she was accustomed to
spending the occasional midweek holiday or snow day with
Ravenna. This branching out
on Ravenna's part, especially towards one of her own good
friends, startled and upset her. I suggested she ask somebody
else. No, she would invite both of them.

Looking at her, I was not sure that was a good idea. At
the same time I marveled at her decision, so different from
what my own would have been: to turn away and pretend
not to care.

Around three-thirty, Jane and I picked up the girls at
Ravenna's house. Happy with the day's play together, they
entered the car eagerly, only to fall silent before Jane's curt
monosyllables. After an uncomfortable ride to the museum,
I walked Ravenna and Lila across the street, saying I wanted
to talk to Jane for a minute. Then I went back and put the
money into the meter, saying firmly, "You don't like friends
to be possessive. It's good for Ravenna to have some other
friends at school. You have."

"Don't you see how she only talks to Lila?"

"I don't care. This was your idea. It's up to you to make it
a success."

Jane hardly paused before looking both ways and skipping
across the street to join the others. Then they all ran together, holding hands, to the museum.

Here in the library with a ceiling fan barely stirring the air and the few desks, poked among the stacks of books, deserted for the air-conditioned section, I glance up from my pages. Ravenna, a popular girl and close friend of both Lila and Jessica, has still maintained her ties to Jane. This summer she came to stay with us for a week on Lupin. Other than a stomachache that disappeared as soon as she saw her mother again, she weathered the visit well. Most of the time the girls kept busy and happy. But one afternoon they were not speaking to each other. Jane had done something wrong and said she was sorry. Ravenna could not forgive her and turned away from her tentative overtures. I observed with difficulty Ravenna's aloofness hurting my child. Did Ravenna, Stella, and I have that quality in common? Kate, my best friend, and I rarely quarreled, but sometimes, in my willingness to please her and keep the peace, I did not speak up. Consequently, at those times I became resentful and withdrew. But Kate, quick-tongued and critical as she could be, was loyal, affectionate, and never aloof.

I looked at the girls' unhappy faces and said, "Do you know what I've learned something about since I was your age? Forgiveness. When I can forgive somebody's else's mistakes, then I can forgive my own more easily." Jane seemed to relax a little, but Ravenna looked down. "But Jane got mad at me when I . . ." She paused. "And when I . . ." She paused again.

"Ravenna," I said, "it's not fair to blame Jane for everything she's done in the past to make you angry. You've got to speak up at the time." And I thought of how I had not, especially to Kate but also to Anne.

"I hurt people when I speak up," Ravenna said, "or I make them angry."

"Try not to be angry or unkind. Just speak up firmly—at the time. It doesn't mean you'll always get your way, but at least you've expressed yourself."

That night when Jane said to Ravenna, "Let's go play in the living room," Ravenna got into bed and said firmly, "I'm tired. I want to go to bed." In trying to follow my advice during the next few days, Ravenna began to frustrate Jane. But by the end of the visit there were signs that they both were happier with each other.

Ironically, just as doubts regarding myself as a parent are beginning to surface, I find I am a better one. When I started writing this book, I thought I had been a perfect mother, and the possibility that I might become less perfect as Jane grew older alarmed me. Now I realize that perfection has no place in my life and never has, other than the restraint its illusion has forced upon me.

I think about the dream in which I was separated from Jane and her friend and about the shocking, sudden drop that appeared before my feet. Did it represent art's ultimate danger: isolation leading if not to death then to numbness? In the dream I instantly turned my back upon the cliff in my frantic haste to find the girls. Yet in the hills I do not remember looking for them but rather for something else. Myself? Only during that search for something else did I happen upon the town and the telephone.

The chapter I have just read over is about endings: Jane's good-bye tea for her teacher, her good-bye to her friends and second grade, my good-bye to Jane as a young child. The next pages are about another good-bye, which deserves a chapter by itself.

43

Homer died a few days before Thanksgiving. The lump grew back in his mouth and became infected. Rather than give him antibiotics so he could survive for a short, increasingly painful spell, we called the vet. She came to our place and gave him a shot. Bob wrapped the body in a sheet and carried it to the vet's car. I envied him the contact, longing to hug Homer one last time.

That is the only feeling of grief I have experienced since his death. But there is a legacy that exists on a muted, daily basis which makes me look at dogs differently. I watch them as I walk around the reservoir, old and young, big, medium, small, this and that breed or mixed breed. I look at them intelligently, and they look at me in the same way. Sometimes one will pause to nudge my hand or lightly brush my leg in passing. Homer, whom I could not stereotype, made dogs real for me.

As he made death. After I called the vet to attend to him, I sat reading, awaiting her arrival with more curiosity than dread, while Homer lay unsuspecting at my feet. In a way I was as unsuspecting as he.

When the needle went in, I was facing him, stroking his head. As quickly as death came, the shock it caused—as if he had been shot—conveyed its magnitude in his eyes. Afterwards, I felt bereaved of both his presence and his trust.

Homer's absence during the workday cast even more of a shadow over Bob. Eventually, he painted a portrait entitled "My Good Friend." Homer's head, neck, and shoulders are placed against a blue sky and almost fill the canvas. His eyes are blue instead of brown, his fur reddish brown, not orange, and he wears a jacket and tie.

During those first weeks without Homer Jane got angry at us more frequently than usual and had trouble going to sleep. We let her drag her air mattress and sleeping bag into our room when she was still awake at our bedtime. From *Between Parent and Child*, a book left out on a sidewalk, I read the following:

> *Emotions are part of our genetic heritage. Fish swim, birds fly, and people feel . . . Emotional education can help children to know what they feel. It is more important for a child to know what he feels than why he feels it. When he knows clearly what his feelings are, he is less likely to feel "all mixed up" inside.*

After a December birthday party Jane brought home a large balloon: Balloony, she called it. For a while, it was a special toy, as Homer's fear of balloons had banned them from home. We played games with it, and she played with it by herself. When it popped several days later, Jane looked at the plastic rag for an instant. Then she cried. Later, she put it into a small, special box and silently showed it to me. It stayed on her bureau for a few weeks.

Christmas passed and then a late New Year's Eve party that included Jane. The following night she attempted a sleepover and returned home as late as she had from the New Year's Eve party. The third night, the one before school opened again, a friend of ours came over and bought a painting from Bob. It was the kind of sale where the painting is loved by the buyer. After the friend left, there was a brief moment of joy in the air, and I hugged Bob. Then I remembered that he had not expressed pleasure in a similar sale of mine some months ago. Instead of confronting him,

I grew quiet and absent-minded. Jane, feeling my mood shift and exhausted after her two late nights, became upset over a minor issue. Or rather, it seemed she was pretending to be upset. I turned on her angrily. She could not fall asleep at her bedtime. Finally, at one in the morning I lay on a sleeping bag beside her bed until she dropped off.

She had begged me to stay with her earlier, but I had refused. I had also insisted she read in her room. I finally let her read on Bob's and my bed while I confronted Bob with the real cause of my anger. He explained that my behavior was frustrating for him. I did not ask enough for my work or try hard enough to sell it. I took so long to finish and finished so little.

The next morning after taking Jane to school, I read in my studio until it was time to pick her up. The late afternoon and evening passed slowly and uneventfully, inspiring reflection.

When sold, the painting from last fall's Open Studios was not quite complete. It was Bob who urged me to get on with it. He even made the frame, as he had several to date, impatience with my tardiness finding some release there. Over the years good art equipment, even a heavy wooden easel, and occasionally a book on an artist whose work I admired were birthday presents meant to help. But his own professionalism and daily efforts as an artist were the real spurs. Gradually, I realized two things. First, his occasional lack of enthusiasm in the past over what I saw as milestones in my work was not so much fear of my success as of my failure—in my eyes a smaller crime.

What about my own worries? One had been the possibility of my success surpassing his. I saw my doctor sitting across his desk from me and saying with a quick smile, "Do you just assume it could? That's not giving him enough credit."

Beyond a certain measure of recognition, however, success

meant something different to Bob and me. Our war in Paris —making money versus saving it—paralleled his urge to sell paintings and mine to save them. I completed an average of one or two paintings a year, if that; Bob, at least fifteen. The number of times I mistakenly thought something was finished made high the risk of selling too soon. As yet, I wanted my work around me to improve, if need be, and to see what was good and bad and where it was going. Since few seemed interested in buying, and my prices were high, so far I was getting my way, failing in the world's and Bob's eyes perhaps but not necessarily my own.

As for writing, was that in order to finish paintings, or out of the hope of reaching a wider audience, or because Bob was not writing? Or was it because I was my mother's child in a way I have denied? As she maintained a stable marriage, raised five children, and completed numerous works of art and writing, so too—apart from the number of children, works, and hours spent working—was I following in her footsteps? Did the need for variety motivate us both, though for many years anxiety compressed and narrowed mine?

Have I denied competition with her, even as I have with Bob, giving her work less credit than is due and so been blind to its real success?

My second realization during the slow afternoon and evening was that I had been wrong to get angry at Jane for her fake tears. I had rubbed signs of grief onto my face before my father's memorial service because I wanted sympathy, even though I did not know or was unable to accept how I felt. The trick, I concluded, was to look for what lay behind the pretense.

That night a blizzard hit. The sound of snowflakes hissing against the window panes woke Jane repeatedly. Each time she would call for me. Finally, at four in the morning, I explained a limit had been reached. She must not disturb me again except for an emergency. When she was a baby, I explained, I went to her because she could not comfort herself. Now she could read or do what she wanted, as long as she did not disturb Bob and me. When I finished speaking, she asked me to turn out the light. She pulled the covers around her and did not call again.

Setting a limit was the solution after all. But the next night I put an exhausted child to bed in good time, the place in order, only to hear her say she knew she would not be able to go to sleep. That was always an ominous, accurate prediction. Defeated, I sat on the side of her bed.

She said she had had a bad dream the night before. Generally reluctant to describe her dreams, she began to tell me about this one. As I listened, I was baffled. Something false again.

"Honey, it won't help you if I sit here all night. You've got to try to solve this problem yourself."

"How?" she asked bleakly.

Earlier in the evening she had cut out of the newspaper an article entitled "What to Do if a Dog Attacks." I had spotted it, and she had decided to choose it for her current events homework assignment due the next day. The article noted, among other things, how many children had been killed by dog attacks, while the accompanying photograph showed a snarling canine face with bared teeth and mean eyes. Jane was starting to write about the article when suddenly she threw down her pencil and refused to go on. Eventually, she wrote the following:

> *My article is about what to do if you are attacked by a dog. Most dogs are not bad. The few that are have often been mistreated. If you are attacked by a dog,* STAY STILL. *Do not run or scream. Remember, if you run, the dog will think you are a chickien (sic) or rabbit.*

Sitting in the darkness on the side of her bed and remembering her throwing down the pencil, I knew that at this moment she was frightened, although not by the dream she had described.

Now and then, I say the Lord's Prayer to her before bed. Addressing Our Father and Mother, I recited it that night. It seems to offer an elementary formula for survival: a safe place, food, forgiveness, avoidance of temptation and evil. And it asks help from a greater power.

I said to Jane, "I believe there was somebody who tried to teach the world about love and its power. I believe love does cast out fear." She was asleep soon after I left the room. She told me the following morning that later in the night she woke up and stayed awake for a long time but did not call.

The next afternoon a neighbor was urging her two aging golden retrievers into her car. One of the dogs lifted its gray muzzle, barked at Jane, and walked quickly over to her. His head came to past her waist, but she was not alarmed and stood still while he sniffed at her. Her face had a friendly, surprised, sweet look upon it. Then the dogs climbed into the car and were taken away for a drive with their mistress.

The Lord's Prayer will not always help but it may provide one defense when fear of life or death threaten to overwhelm her. Although Homer was not a child's dog, his presence was part of the central order of her world, and its removal exposed her for the first time to a potential chaos that angered and frightened her. And it was a dog who carried the bad news. If Homer could die, so could she, or Bob, or I, or anybody. And dogs not only could die but could kill her—even Homer had had the ability to do so—like a chicken or rabbit, or as we, her parents, had killed Homer.

Jane stopped to talk to Star Tree, a tree she had picked out to confide in over the past couple of years, half believing in it, half not. I walked on, thinking about the two old dogs.

They would die soon or be killed if their mistress deemed life was too painful for them.

This winter I had had to wait a few weeks for a repeat medical test. Visiting my friend Kate for a weekend shortly before my return appointment, I mentioned it to her. We were about to sit down to supper: a fragrant, delicious-appearing meal she had just cooked. "It's probably nothing," she said, referring to the test, "but it must bother you." Then in surprise, "You're tested only once a year? My doctor recommends every six months." Suddenly, I had no appetite.

The test turned out fine. But walking past Jane and her tree, I thought about that loss of appetite and about endings. Finishing a painting is like dying in a small way, as necessary to face as the final letting go. I have balked and balked, denying smaller endings and the larger one until paralysis —similar to what overtook me when I first realized Homer was going to die soon—might eventually have overtaken my ability to work.

When I finish a painting, for a short interval I am filled with the joy of achievement and the hope that even as the work interested me, it may interest others. Then the intensity of both the joy and hope lessen, and the void surrounds me. In the future, made more capable and loving by what I have completed, I will reach across it to my social ties.

Although it is winter now, I think of the different kinds of flowers growing in our neighborhood during the warmer months. The roses stand for the art of loving, in which I am not so far behind others as I have supposed.

A marigold rises over its dark leaves like the sun over Flamingo's silhouetted treetops. But first come the calls from the island roosters that woke me as a child and embodied my eagerness for the day ahead.

The pale gladiola is my father's middle-aged ghost greeting me on certain mornings when I awake and premonitions of loss and unfinished work wrap themselves like fog around me, and only the day's gray duties lie ahead.

The dark purple carnations on their long, smooth, milky green stems, even as they beckon, are an overnight letter from Bob when I was by myself on Lupin last summer and lonely: "I hope you will enjoy a few days of solitude without any responsibilities...painting, writing?" Then an after-thought in pencil, "(But those are great responsibilities.)"

The deep, deep purple-blue iris are my night dreams that I miss. The edge of change is beginning to pass, and my memory no longer taps into them as vividly or often as it did.

44

Earlier this month Stella invites me to a ladies' supper. I arrive, casually dressed and expecting a party of four or five, to be greeted by a formal, annual affair consisting of perhaps thirty professional women I do not know. Stella introduces me around as a writer who has just finished a book. Another night I would have corrected her immediately. Instead, thrown off balance by the difference between my expectations for the evening and what it is, I begin to tell each person I am introduced to that "No, I haven't finished it yet. As a matter of fact, I'm not really a writer," and so forth. A novelist informs me she is starting a book over from scratch for the third time. A woman with a grant to research a topic of interest to herself claims that getting published is as rare as winning the lottery. At the dinner table the new guests are each encouraged to talk about what they are doing. I am specifically asked to talk about the book, which I do. I think nothing can shake my faith in it, unfinished as it is, even talking to a roomful of strangers about it. When I return home, I say to Bob in despair, "I was so foolish."

I sleep poorly for the next couple of nights and one afternoon eat a box of chocolates, a present I planned to give to a friend. A sore throat that has lasted nearly a month and vanished the day before the supper returns. On the third morning I awake in the early hours and, unable to go back to sleep, retire to the living room sofa. It has been unusually cold. Just outside the living room windows a street lamp whitens bare branches and the empty pavement below.

Further back, it shines more dimly on a road leading into the neighborhood where I took a late walk before bed. A lonely wilderness had swelled under the surfaces of things, making them appear flimsy and one-dimensional.

I look restlessly away from the windows, back into the living room. A large black-and-white photograph from our basement storeroom stands on a table nearby, leaning against the wall. Bob wants to get it framed with my mother's Christmas money. For a long time I stare at its aerial view of some islands in Maine—including Lupin and its barred relative—and note their rough shapes, darker in the middle with trees, lighter around their edges and points, wherever the rocks and shrubbery are. The smaller, treeless islands are lightest of all. The expanse of sea, as dark as the trees, is broken on the left by a semicircular piece of the sun's reflection on minuscule waves. The island I know so well by walking and rowing around is entirely different from the air. How can I know things so intimately on some levels and hardly at all on others? Yet seen that way from a bird's eye, high up and with no color, only different shades of gray, the falling islands and sea convey the familiar essence of that dangerous, beautiful expanse of space. It reminds me of another airy reach I saw from Flamingo's lighthouse long ago: not gray but white, pale blue, and yellow.

As I stare at the photograph, I begin to relax. The light from the lamp next to the sofa, reaching as far as the photograph, centers on my lap. I draw my legs up close into its bright circle. Furniture, lamps, and pictures bunch together in the shadows and form abstract shapes.

The dinner party comes to mind. Why had I felt foolish afterwards? Had I been stupid, or had I missed the overall view? I try to examine the different sources of my discomfort. Stella encouraged me to expose myself and my unfinished writing to strangers, albeit her friends. I did so, nervous at first but at no point reluctant. The book was what I was presently obsessed with, not my paintings. What I said about it was accurate, not foolish.

What about the foolishness of talking publicly about a thing not yet completed, perhaps never to be? In my mind I look back and see a theme running through the manuscript's pages, connecting solitary work with my social self. Sometimes it runs as straight and white as the road from my childhood town to the lighthouse; at other times as circular and gray as the sea's route from island to island. How have I found it? By not looking for it and by letting an urgency born of unfinished work and loneliness point me in its direction. And talking before Stella's friends provided at the least one impetus to continue.

That afternoon Amy happened to tell me about a talk show she had listened to on the radio, and she concluded, "Sometimes, I think there is no sense of privacy left in the world."

"I hate to think what I would say on one of those shows," I say. We both laughed.

On my sofa in the early morning hours, I smile and think briefly of Amy. Then, of Stella and of what she and her party have given me. Finally, my mind empties itself. The photograph begins to change. At first it resembles an x-ray. Then, the downward pointing islands followed by the smaller bits of land become falling stars trailing light in the blackness of space. I switch off the lamp and go to bed.

45

Remember that argument about confidence I avoided having with my brother, Steven, the summer before Jane entered second grade? It is springtime, almost two years later, and he is with me now. He has stopped by on his way to an East Coast business meeting. We walk around the reservoir together with our jackets opened and the last bits of snow melting. Our argument, or rather discussion as it turns out to be, begins not with how we and our mother were brought up, but with the cow jumping over the moon.

Steven: Instead of the cow who jumped over the moon, pretend there was a cow who thought it could jump over the moon, but as much as it practiced, it couldn't. Do you think that cow would be a confident cow? Interesting, but not confident.

And there is always the world in which the cow lives. Suppose the cow's efforts are fantastic, or suppose she does jump over the moon. Perhaps the world thinks jumping over the moon is foolish and unimportant, or that only bulls should jump over the moon—not cows. Do you think that cow would be confident, successful or not?

Steven paused, maybe thinking of the time he left his business to be his children's primary caretaker. His neighbors had exhibited a marked lack of respect for his new occupation.

Me: Then the cow must decide which is more important, the world's opinion or her own. If the latter, I suspect she could find at least a few others who could appreciate her feat. The little dog did—in a way—and the dish and the spoon.

Steven: And lastly, the world might overrate the cow's jump, and the cow might feel the world admired her only for that.

Me to myself, putting my pencil down and stepping outside my book for a minute: A human being has not yet jumped over the moon, but a machine of human design has taken men over it and more than one man has walked on it. Amazing. And amazing that my book began with a name: Persus. Persis was a friend of a cousin. Out of the blue she invited me to tea. Hannah was in second grade then. Early spring afternoon. Persis about fifty, repainting her apartment herself. Didn't even own it. Mediterranean colors, oranges and pinks. Lush like the tea. Cakes, fruits, cheese, home-made bread. I decided to write a book about Persus, a girl. I was walking home from the tea. Faith, I mean Kate, read the first, second, and third draft. About the first she said, "Parts of this are boring. It seems to me you want to write about yourself." With each draft I wrote more about myself, but Persus stayed. Not Persis, but Persus. Friends wanted to know why I chose that name: "Persus' socks" was difficult to read aloud... there weren't many women's rights in Persia ... instead of Persus, why not Mary, Emma, Sophie? Several times I changed Persus' name only to change it back. Finally, I knew why it gave birth to the book: Persus... PURSUIT. By then the book was mine, and Persus, no longer standing for what I pursued, turned easily into Jane.

Me to Steven: I've been writing a book. Each chapter, like the book itself, was a leap in the dark. I had no idea where I was going or how things would end, but I felt compelled to leap. As the moon's light may have guided the cow and its gravity pulled her, so something guided and pulled me.

Steven: What started you writing?

Me: I couldn't seem to finish paintings.

Steven: Can you now?

Me: Not yet, at least not any more than before. But maybe what I was after isn't so much the point.

Steven: What is?

Me: I don't know.

Steven: What's the book about?

Me: Me, as I've just described to you, and finding things, like certain aspects of myself as a mother, daughter, sister, wife, friend, and artist.

Steven: What aspects?

Me: Social ones. I mean social in the sense of being able to connect with others in a positive way.

Steven: As opposed to being an artist?

Me: Not as opposed to. The opposite, really. Actually, that's one of the things I discover.

Steven: But in the beginning you didn't know what you were writing about?

Me: No, I didn't. If I wanted to write about something badly enough, I did, and one thing led to another. Then one draft led to another. I was into a much later draft before I realized what I was writing about. But from the beginning to end, before I found anything, I had to let go. That usually meant writing about something with no apparent rationale besides wanting to. But sometimes it meant turning away from something I considered most important to something secondary, in order to find the primary thing. Then I'd discover what seemed secondary wasn't less significant at all.

Steven: So there was this overall, circular process. What did you find?

Me: My fears on different social fronts.

Steven: What social fronts?

Me: Ones related to being a wife, mother, artist, daughter, friend, sibling, granddaughter.

Steven: Did those insecurities boil down to anything?

Me: Daddy's death, I guess. He was your age when he

died. It took writing the book for me to realize that he was a perfectionist and romantic like me. He died because of what he was, and my insecurities or fears stem from what I am.

Steven: Do you think he actually died because of what he was? That's like saying we bring on our own deaths. Of course we do sometimes, but Daddy may have had a defective heart or something else physically wrong that had nothing to do with the way he lived his life. He was discouraged, but I don't think he wanted to die.

Me: All right, let's say he didn't. But his sense of failure during the second half of his life stemmed from what he was. So, I guess my fears come down to Daddy's sense of failure rather than his death. By writing the book, maybe I have found a way out: how to temper what I am.

Steven: How?

Me: By replacing isolationism with interconnectedness. We were talking about confidence. Feeling the interconnectedness of my different roles, for instance, gives me confidence, the kind I need to let go and find things.

Steven: For example...

Me: After I revised the book a number of times, I still wasn't satisfied with its organization. I tried lumping the chapters together under the headings Mother, Artist, Wife, Daughter, and so on. The book died. Lumping them together instead of leaving them interspersed throughout the book, as they had been written, drastically reduced the one-thing-leading-to-another element. It cut the thread of interconnectedness that had moved the search forward.

Steven: How did you fix things?

Me: When the book died, I realized what had given it life. I interspersed the chapters even more than they had been written—closer to how they first came to mind—and that solved the organization problem by emphasizing what gave the book life.

Steven: I see.

Me: Take the cow jumping over the moon. I think the world pays more attention to her jump than to the cat fiddling, the dog laughing, and the dish running away with the spoon. At least I did. But now I see it as inseparable from the presence of the others: the cat with its fiddle, the dog, the dish, and the spoon. The earth's surface, left and returned to, is as necessary as the depth of the surrounding space, the quiet of outer space as the music of the fiddle. All are part of the cow's jump and as important. The interconnectedness of those different things helps it to happen.

In "Hey, Diddle, Diddle" you can see and hear the connections between the words themselves. And their meaning is equally connected. The overall connection that poetry often has is the kind of connection I'm talking about.

Steven: How is it all related to confidence?

Me: When I realize that everything is connected, my self is no longer so important. Both my successes and failures are less my own. They are more varied. As the world cannot grasp entirely who or what goes into them, what the world thinks is less important. I am less this and that, more part of this and that.

A few years ago when I thought I was failing as an artist, I dreamt I had no center. My head, arms, and legs had flown off in all different directions. Now my center of confidence isn't only as an artist, or even as a friend, daughter, sibling, writer, mother, wife, granddaughter, artist but as a friend-granddaughterwriterwifeartistmothersiblingdaughter, or even as a tgdneiuwdrafsdhetgbtreiaafrlgrteiwlorgtrrenihretnsmaduhi. Since I've begun to look at other people in the same way, they interest me more and overwhelm me less than they used to.

Steven: I see.

Me: When Jane wants to dance with me, she asks me to change into tights and a leotard because they will help me feel like it. They do, Jane and I have fun dancing. Having fun together is one aspect of being a good parent, don't you think? We might dance to the beat of a nursery rhyme, "Hey, Diddle, Diddle," for example. The next day, you and I might take a walk and discuss confidence using that nursery rhyme as a metaphor. Our discussion strengthens our ties as siblings. Later, I might write a chapter in which we talk about confidence using "Hey, Diddle, Diddle" as a metaphor. Who created my chapter? Me, you, Jane, the creator of the nursery rhyme, the maker of the tights, the moon. See, it's all connected. That connection gives me the confidence to let go. Letting go helps me find things and along the way finish books and paintings.

Me thinking to myself: There is the moon (the one the cow jumped over and humans walked on) high in the afternoon sky, reflecting the light of the earth as I too often reflected the light of other people's wishes. Here I am walking around the reservoir by myself in the springtime, no Steven with me after all, feeling high as the moon over possibilities.

Shortly after that walk I met a gallery director on the street. I had once shown in a group show at the gallery of a now retired colleague of hers.

"How's the painting going?" she asked.

"This winter I've been writing instead of painting," I admitted reluctantly. "But I'll be painting again soon."

She shrugged and smiled at me. "It's nearly the same thing, isn't it? Come see me when you have some work for me to look at."

A studio artist for thirty-four years, the author lives in Cambridge, Massachusetts with her husband, daughter, and dog. *Finding Bob's Glasses* is her first book.